Managing Cultural Differences

Strategies for Competitive Advantage

The EIU Series

This innovative series of books is the result of a publishing collaboration between Addison-Wesley and the Economist Intelligence Unit. Our authors draw on the results of original research by the EIU's skilled research and editorial staff to provide a range of topical, information-rich and incisive business titles. They are specifically tailored to the needs of international executives and business education worldwide.

Titles in the Series

Cauley de la Sierra	*Managing Global Alliances: Key Steps for Successful Collaboration*
Daniels	*Information Technology: The Management Challenge*
Egan and McKiernan	*Inside Fortress Europe: Strategies for the Single Market*
Irons	*Managing Service Companies: Strategies for Success*
Manser	*Control from Brussels*
Maxton and Wormald	*Driving Over A Cliff? Business Lessons from the World's Car Industry*
Mazur and Hogg	*The Marketing Challenge*
Paliwoda	*Investing in Eastern Europe: Capitalizing on Emerging Markets*
Underwood	*Intelligent Manufacturing*
White and Mazur	*Strategic Communications Management: Making Public Relations Work*

Managing Cultural Differences

Strategies for Competitive Advantage

Lisa Hoecklin

The Economist
Intelligence Unit

ADDISON-WESLEY PUBLISHING COMPANY

Wokingham, England • Reading, Massachusetts • Menlo Park, California • New York
Don Mills, Ontario • Amsterdam • Bonn • Sydney • Singapore
Tokyo • Madrid • San Juan • Milan • Paris • Mexico City • Seoul • Taipei

© 1995 Addison-Wesley Publishers Ltd, Addison-Wesley Publishing Co. Inc. and the Economist Intelligence Unit

This book uses material drawn from the Report, *Managing Cultural Differences for Competitive Advantage*, first published by Economist Intelligence Unit.

Cover designed by Viva Design Ltd, Henley-on-Thames
incorporating photograph by Theresa Thompson
and printed by The Riverside Printing Co. (Reading) Ltd.
Text designed by Valerie O'Donnell.
Line diagrams drawn by Margaret Macknelly Design, Tadley.
Typeset by Meridian Phototypesetting Limited, Pangbourne.
Printed in Great Britain at the University Press, Cambridge.

First printed 1994. Reprinted 1995.

ISBN 0-201-42770-2

British Library Cataloguing in Publication Data
A catalogue record for this book is available from the British Library.

Library of Congress Cataloging in Publication Data applied for.

Contents

Overview   *ix*

**1   The impact of cultural diversity on international
      business**   **1**
   Are cultures converging?   2
      Box 1.1: What is a considerate supervisor?   3
   The costs of cultural mismanagement   5
   Culture affects even 'ordinary' business practices   7
   Are there universal management theories?   8
      Box 1.2: The idea of separate categories or 'modes' of thought   9
   Morality is a movable feast   10
   Perceptions of other cultures: USA – Europe   11
      Box 1.3: An American executive in Paris   12
   Creating a global organization out of diversity   15
   The competitive advantage of culture   15
      Case 1.1: Using culture competitively at ICI   18
   Summary   21
   References   21

**2   Culture: what it is, what it is not and how it
      directs organizational behaviour**   **23**
   What culture is   24
   What culture is not   25
   Different layers of culture   25
   Definitions of culture   27
   Attempts to classify national culture in terms of the importance
   attached to different values   27
      Box 2.1: Concepts of culture by some of the gurus   28
      Box 2.2: Hofstede's four dimensions of culture-related values   29

Box 2.3: Difference in work ethos between an individualist
and a collectivist society   37
Fons Trompenaars's research   40
Box 2.4: Trompenaars's country abbreviations   40
Culture and Dutchmen   47
Summary   48
References   48

3 **The strategic value of cultural differences**   **50**
Competitive requirements of internationalization   50
Creating sustainable sources of competitive advantage   52
Approaches to managing cultural differences   53
Four strategies for managing cultural differences   56
Case 3.1: Ikea   57
Case 3.2: Elf Aquitaine   63
Case 3.3: Emerson Electric   65
Case 3.4: Bührmann-Tetterode   70
Asia/Pacific models of organization   71
The competitive advantage of cultures   74
Case 3.5: Siemens   77
Box 3.1: Cultural learning disabilities   79
A model of cultural learning   80
Case 3.6: Cultural learning at Toshiba in the UK   81
Case 3.7: Cultural learning at Toshiba in the USA   84
Case 3.8: Cultural learning at Toyota in the USA   85
A value-added perspective on managing across cultures   89
Summary   90
References   91

4 **Advertising across cultures**   **92**
Do 'global' products exist?   92
Box 4.1: Critical lessons from early international marketing
experiences   93
Global products, global meanings?   94
Box 4.2: Views on global marketing   96
Case 4.1: Heineken beer – brewing a global brand   102
Box 4.3: The impact of culture on market research   104
Case 4.2: Johnson & Johnson baby products – the language
of love   105
A value-added approach to marketing and advertising across
cultures   106
Case 4.3: Unilever's fish-fingers   108
Case 4.4: Unisys Corporation – translating customer service
into a global message   109
Case 4.5: Steelcase Strafor   110
Summary   111
References   112

5   Managing human resources across cultures   **113**

The context   114
Articulating explicit company values worldwide   116
   Box 5.1: Lotus – basic values   117
   Box 5.2: Motorola – basic values and objectives   118
   Box 5.3: Basic commitment of the Toshiba Group   119
'Every act of creation is an act of destruction'   120
Selection   122
Career development   125
Performance appraisal   131
The role of HRM professionals in a multicultural world   133
Summary   134
References   135

6   Managing alliances across cultures   **136**

Strategic rationale for alliances   136
   Box 6.1: East European managers accuse Westerners of
   aggressiveness   137
   Box 6.2: Recommendations for successful cross-border
   alliances   138
The role of culture in alliances across cultures   139
   Case 6.1: Joint venture between Motorola and Toshiba   140
The interaction between national and corporate culture   145
   Box 6.3: Cultural comparisons between a Californian
   high-tech company and its European subsidiary   147
   Case 6.2: Acquisition of Kyat (Spanish) by Syseca (French)   150
   Box 6.4: Cultural approaches to negotiations   151
Managing the process   151
References   153

Index   *155*

Overview

People are increasingly having to interact, manage, negotiate and compromise with people from other cultures. The potential for management frustration, costly misunderstandings and even business failures increases significantly when dealing with people whose values, beliefs, customs and first language are different from your own. However, when understood and successfully managed, differences in culture can lead to innovative business practices and sustainable sources of competitive advantage.

In a global marketplace, many leading international business scholars are arguing, the more sustainable competitive advantages are increasingly changing from 'harder' efficiency sources to 'softer' effectiveness sources. For example, moving to a low-cost labour area is a replicable, short-term advantage. The more sustainable advantages are firm-specific abilities working in an international context, building flexibility, sharing information and developing collective know-how into a worldwide network. Faster and better learning within organizations is a large part of the evolving competitive logic. In order to develop these capabilities, people from different cultures have to be able to communicate, negotiate, compromise and understand each other's values and world views.

Furthermore, there are balances to be struck in the continuing process of globalization, such as developing global economies of scale and at the same time being responsive to local environments; nurturing diversity and at the same time needing integration; maintaining flexibility and at the same time being focused. These are issues with which each organization and function struggles on the road to globalization. Understanding the role of culture is of utmost relevance in resolving these dilemmas.

This book's research findings help bring clarity to what can appear a 'fuzzy' area of international management. The evidence seems broadly to reveal that:

- The impact of national culture differences is relevant to all areas of a global business;
- Globally operating companies have used different strategies to manage cultural differences;
- Some of these strategies are now inappropriate to emerging organizational structures and competitive requirements;
- There are many more examples of companies articulating their intention to use cultural diversity for competitive advantage at a strategic level then there are successful examples at an operational level.

While there are no clear-cut or universal 'answers' on how to manage cultural differences for each business area of this book, for all of the reasons that will be outlined in Chapter 1, it is possible to explore the impact of culture on each area and provide frameworks for considering cultural factors. By learning something about the variety of human cultures, and about how that variety affects people's approach to business, it is possible to see that your own solutions may not be the only, the best or the most appropriate for the task at hand. It is this basic realization that is the first step in using cultural differences strategically.

Acknowledgements

I should like to gratefully acknowledge the contributions of Paul Thorne and Eveline Vermeulen. Both provided valuable ideas, experience and case studies. Special thanks also to the many executives from all of the companies covered in the text – in Europe, the USA and Japan – who spent several hours discussing their experiences and perspectives on managing cultural differences strategically.

The book would not have happened at all without the trust and encouragement of three people. Carolyn White believed in and supported the initial project at the Economist Intelligence Unit, Tim Pitts at Addison-Wesley provided the opportunity to turn the material into a book, and my husband, Peter, was as always a constant source of ideas and enthusiasm.

Lisa Hoecklin
October 1994

1

The impact of cultural diversity on international business

As markets, competition and organizations globalize, the business-people, politicians and consumers who comprise these institutions are increasingly having to interact, manage, negotiate and compromise with people from different cultures. Working with people whose values and beliefs, not to mention languages and customs, are very different from your own can make for costly misunderstandings and even business failures. As hard experience has made international managers and politicians painfully aware, business and politics are not discrete, rational domains of activity separate from a society's particular cultural beliefs and values. All social behaviour is embedded in a particular context and is connected to other deeply held values and beliefs. This means that the stakes are high for mismanaging cultural differences. Ignoring or mishandling differences can mean inability to retain and motivate employees, misreading the potential of cross-border alliances, marketing and advertising blunders, and failure to build sustainable sources of competitive advantage. Mismanaging cultural differences can render otherwise successful managers and organizations ineffective and frustrated when working across cultures. When successfully managed, however, differences in culture can lead to innovative business practices, faster and better learning within the organization, and sustainable sources of competitive advantage.

Although this is clearly an area of increasing importance in international business, it is also an enormously difficult subject to research (Redding, 1992). Besides the high cost of international organizational research there are the methodological issues of trying to separate the

1

myriad of determinants. For example, how much of organizational behaviour is influenced by the national culture of its members? How much is specific to the uniqueness of its corporate culture or the industry or technology? How can we account for the fact that researchers will inevitably have their own cultural biases which can affect the way they design and conduct their research? As is the case in most complex fields, useful theory is lagging behind the pace at which globally operating companies are encountering the impact of cultural differences. This book is intended to help students of international business and strategic thinkers in multinational organizations come to terms with the importance of national cultural differences in organizations and to provide some practical insights and frameworks in order to manage these differences more successfully.

First, however, it is necessary to consider the trend that some would argue diminishes the importance of national culture in international business; that is, the so-called convergence of cultures.

Are cultures converging?

There are a number of scholars who argue that modernization will create or at least lead to a common culture worldwide. This would make the life of international managers much simpler. While there are, indeed, many products, services and even holidays becoming common to world markets – McDonald's, Coca-Cola, sushi, credit cards and Christmas – that does not mean that these things have the same meaning in different cultures. Dining at McDonald's is a show of status in Moscow, whereas in New York all it means is a fast meal for a fast buck (Trompenaars, 1993). Christmas as a festival has the potential of becoming the epitome of globalization yet it is its very ability to symbolize so many different things, to combine or reconcile differing beliefs, which makes its adoption across cultures possible. In every place it becomes the protector and legitimation for specific regional and particular customs and traditions. In Japan it has come to symbolize youth, romantic love and 'dating'. In Trinidad the festival is centred around the home and domesticity. In the UK, Christmas is a celebration of the immediate family and its continuity. The American holiday focuses on celebrating friends, family and the community. While the superficial events of Christmas may seem homogeneous – people overeat and overspend – Christmas may be merely a façade for quite heterogeneous events (Miller, 1993). In short, the fact that we can all listen to Walkmans, eat hamburgers and visit Santa Claus at a shopping centre only tells us that there are some novel products that can be sold on a universal message. It does not tell us what they mean in the different cultures where they are visible.

If globally operating companies want their philosophies, objectives, products and services to be not only understood but also believed by employees, customers and partners in different cultures, they must attend to what these things *mean* to the people in each culture. However objective or uniform we try to make organizations, they will not have the same meaning for individuals from different cultures. It is quite possible that an organization can be the same in such objective dimensions as physical plant, equipment and layout, yet have totally different meanings which various human cultures read into their existence. Similarly, social technologies, like matrix structures, reward systems, performance appraisal, empowerment or consultative management, may seem uniform, but will have very different meanings to individuals from different cultures. It all depends on the cultural context.

Box 1.1   What is a considerate supervisor?

A recent study surveyed leadership behaviours in electronics assembly plants in four countries (Smith and Bond, 1993). The plants were in the USA, Hong Kong, Japan and the UK. In all the plants studied, supervisors who were considerate towards members of the work team were positively evaluated. The focus of the study, however, was on what the supervisor actually has to do to be perceived as considerate. Workers in the plant were asked to indicate how often their supervisors performed a variety of different behaviours. It was found that 'considerate' supervisors have to do rather different things in order to earn that label in each of the different countries. For example, one question asked about what the supervisor might do if a member of the work team is experiencing personal difficulties. Workers in Japan and in Hong Kong responded that to discuss the matter with other members of the work team in the person's absence would be a considerate behaviour. In contrast, workers in the USA and in the UK evaluated such public discussion as an inconsiderate thing to do. Thus the study illustrates how a specific action may have quite different meanings attributed to it depending upon the cultural context within which it is performed. In Japan and Hong Kong greater value is attached to indirect communication as a form of tactfulness, whereas in the UK and the USA higher value is given to directness.

(*Source*: Smith P. B. and Bond M. H. (1993). *Social Psychology Across Cultures: Analysis and Perspectives*, London: Harvester Wheatsheaf)

The essence of culture is not what is visible on the surface. It is the shared ways groups of people understand and interpret the world. These differing interpretations that cultures give to their environment are crucial influences on interactions between people working and managing across cultures.

As superficial behaviour converges, cultural differences accentuate

Far from internationalization leading to cultures becoming more similar, much of the research into culture (and, indeed, the wave of nationalistic sentiments that have vividly and violently emerged in the past few years) reveals that, as some of the superficial aspects of consumer behaviour converge, the more people tend more vigorously to cling to their own culture. Of several dimensions of cultural variation which have been researched (these are detailed in Chapter 2), only one seems to have any correlation with modernization (as measured by per capita GNP). Some studies have shown that increasing prosperity as brought through industrialization has led to an increase in individualism. Concern for personal achievement and ambition gains ascendency over group or community loyalties. The nature of the relationship between industrialization and individualism, though, is as yet unclear and in some studies is small. It appears that other value differences between cultures are free to vary in a number of ways independent of a country's level of modernization (Smith and Bond, 1993).

A 1980 study conducted by André Laurent of INSEAD business school in France, found that French, German and British managers working for an American multinational had values and behaviours *more French, more German and more British* than those of their compatriots working for local, domestic companies (Laurent, 1983). In other words, the more experience these managers had with another culture's way of doing things, the greater their identification with their own cultural beliefs.

In fact, it appears that increasing contact and economic interdependence of nations is convincing many business leaders of the need to maintain their unique cultural values and identities. Hari Bedi, a Hong Kong-based consultant, conducted personal interviews with numerous Asian business leaders about this issue (Hari Bedi, 1991). These executives' perceptions reinforced the notion that, as Western business practices are introduced, there is an increasing emphasis on maintaining your own unique cultural values.

> Paron Israsena, president of the Siam Cement Group in Thailand, explained that although his company offers many managers the opportunity to study at leading foreign business schools, their Thai values are deeply felt. 'We concentrate on

Thai qualities and adapt the techniques and practices we learn from overseas education to the Thai situation,' he said.

When asked if some of the qualities such as *kreng chai* (consideration for the feelings and wishes of others) and *bunkhun* (reciprocating a favour) would not be lost as his company becomes more international, he answered 'Ah, a very good question! We are born with *kreng chai* and *bunkhun*. They are inside our heart. But inevitably in the future the cultures from Europe and the USA will come in and mix. But we are not afraid that we will lose our values. The majority of Thai managers – more than 95% – are typically Thai.' He was convinced it would remain so.

Anthropological work has shown the incredible resilience of cultural groups to adapt to external and internal change in unique ways. Certainly colonialization did not have the same cultural consequences in any one place. You need only to look at Japan's long history of going overseas to learn from other cultures and bringing that learning home to adopt and adapt in order to understand how technical and economic modernization does not necessarily lead to the same changes in cultural profile. Since the middle of the fourth century outside knowledge in Japan was primarily imported from China and Korea. The process of adopting foreign elements involved three stages:

(1) Simple reproduction
(2) Adjustment and modification
(3) Refinement or 'Japanization'.

From the Meiji period onward, ideas and information from Europe were incorporated in the same way. This unique process of 'Japanization' has made it possible for culturally alien but sought-after ideas and practices to become reinterpreted in terms of what are perceived as more 'traditional' Japanese values.

The costs of cultural mismanagement

Increasing management contact and interdependence across cultures are inevitable. Cultural differences are not going away, but becoming more entrenched. This makes it more critical than ever to try to understand different cultures and their influence on the ways people do business and view the world. The costs of not understanding are getting greater and greater. However, all too often in recent years the business press has reported cases where differences in culture have caused otherwise sound deals to go wrong.

CMB, the Anglo-French merger of Metal Box Company and Carnaud in 1989, seemed an excellent strategic fit. Carnaud was strong in France, Germany, Italy and Spain, while Metal Box was the leader in the British market, with some Italian activity. At the time of the merger, the companies were predicted to raise profits to Fr1.9 billion on sales of Fr32 billion by 1993. As of the end of 1991, though, the trend was downward. Most industry experts blamed the failure on 'clash of cultures' at the top level of the company leading to indecision about organization and strategy. One analyst summarizing the CMB situation observed 'management styles are, unfortunately, different throughout Europe and present, therefore, a formidable limitation to European corporate integration... Of course, there are also differences between companies in the same country, but none as great as the cross-country differences.' (Manchau, 1991)

Another costly disaster occurred when a British company tried to lure Italian customers for its *British* products, using *British* marketing techniques. The customers did not bite.

A large British insurance company bought a 50% stake in three small Italian companies in 1989 and proceeded to change their policies to conform with its British products. It thought that standardization was critical. Then the company tried to market them via direct mail and through the branches of its partners in northern Italy. Few policies sold, and the joint venture suffered a pre-tax loss of approximately $90 million in just over one year. (*Institutional Investor*, 1991)

Even among internationally knowledgeable companies that success-fully adapt marketing and sales techniques across cultures, there is often great difficulty recognizing that the things that motivate, inspire and generate commitment depend on each individual's culture of origin.

A large American electrical company with significant foreign operations acquired a French concern. The dismal first-year performance of the new acquisition was thought to be partly due to a poorly motivated sales and marketing staff. The American parent organized a high-tech motivational road show, complete with T-shirts printed with the company slogan for all participants to wear during the three-day event in Paris. The French employ-ees were appalled at the idea of wearing such a 'costume' and indeed, from their perspective, at the way in which the 'vulgar hype' was expected to be motivational. Results of the next two quarters were worse than ever. (*Wall Street Journal*, 1990)

Similarly, an American computer company prepared its '11 Operating Principles' to be distributed to each of its subsidiaries world-wide to ensure that all employees would share a common corporate philosophy. Last on the list was 'HAVE FUN!'. The reaction of Dutch employees was a decided 'They should mind their own business! How dare they tell us what to do!' (Trompenaars, 1993).

Culture affects even 'ordinary' business practices

There are also numerous cases of culture getting in the way of ordinary business practices. Even the ways in which meetings are run, decisions made, memos written and titles used will vary depending on the culture.

Sam Heltman, head of human resources for Toyota Motor Manufacturing in Kentucky (USA), explained how American managers initially misinterpreted the behaviour of Japanese managers they worked with.

> 'Initially some people thought that the Japanese managers were picking apart their proposals and even perhaps being overly critical. But what we didn't realize at the time was that if you go to Japanese managers and ask their opinion about a proposal you've given them, if they *don't* give you something they're going to feel that they haven't done what you've asked of them. So even if they have to struggle to think of something, they'll come up with a suggestion.
>
> 'As a manager, I was more accustomed that if someone brought me a recommendation and if I was 95% ok with it, I bought it just to make them feel good. It's just the opposite for them. If they didn't say something, they would think that you would feel that it wasn't important to them.'

Tadao Taguchi, chairman and chief executive officer of Toshiba America Inc., explains that even the difference between Japan and the USA in addressing business letters reveals a great deal about their ways of viewing the world.

> 'In the USA, you first put the individual's status (Mr or Ms, and so on), then their first name and then last name. The next line is the company name, then the person's title. Next comes the address, city, state and finally the country.

'In Japan, it is the opposite. First comes the country, then the city and address. Next you put the company name, followed by the last name of the individual to whom you are writing. The last thing is the individual's name.'

This example is illustrative on two levels. In the USA, individuals identify primarily with being an individual and *then* with their family, company, religion or some other larger group. In Japan, it is the opposite. Individuals identify primarily with a collectivity – their larger national group, the company they work for, their family – and then with being an individual. Consider the fact that the nearest word to 'I' in the Japanese language translates roughly as 'self among others'.

Mr Taguchi's example also illustrates another difference in the two cultures' approaches to solving problems. The Japanese tend to be more synthetic and holistic in approaching problems, whereas Anglo-Saxon cultures tend to break a problem down into pieces and then work back towards a whole (Hampden-Turner and Trompenaars, 1993; Doktor, 1990).

The basis of these differences will be explored in the next chapter. It is the ineffectiveness of ordinary business practices in a different culture, though, that casts doubt on the usefulness of thinking about management as a set of 'truths' that can be applied uniformly anywhere in the world. If everyday business practices are so culturally dependent, how universal can other, more sophisticated management practices be?

Are there universal management theories?

Most models of the organization and many of the fundamental principles of management studied not only in the West but throughout the world were developed primarily in the USA. The basis of the theories is Anglo-Saxon, and involves very particular assumptions about science, technology, human behaviour and research. The whole notion of organizations as machines, with human beings as 'resources' like physical and monetary resources, is a cultural belief not shared by many other cultures. Similarly, much of the West's regard for management as a profession, where emotionally detached rationality is 'scientifically' necessary, is also a very particular world view. In fact, the distinction between science and non-science and the separation of rational thought as a 'mode of thought' or 'mentality' distinct from emotion, religion, morality and nature, appear to be peculiar to Western thought (Winch, 1970).

Box 1.2   The idea of separate categories or 'modes' of thought

According to the Japanese author Nagashima, most Japanese appear to believe that the Western way of thinking is radically different from their own. The opposing attributes he notes are for the West: objective, analytical, logical, consistent, impersonal, absolute and intellectual. For the East, attributes include: subjective, synthetic, non-logical, inconsistent, personal, relative and emotional. He sums up the value differences in terms of the logical and scientific versus the instinctive and subjective. The rigid distinction between rationality and non-rationality is unique to the West whereas in the Japanese word *omoi*, both elements are integrated and indistinguishable (Nagashima, 1973).

Another interesting comparison comes from Kakir. He says that in India, people's thinking tends to be more representational and affective, relying more on visual and sensual images than on the abstract and conceptual. Compared with Western children, he thinks Indian children are encouraged to live in a mythical, magical world for a long time, where nature, objects, events and other people are intimately related to themselves. This is in sharp contrast to the task of 'individuation' in identity formation in the West. In this view, the self is encased; separated from others and from nature. Then the self is further split into smaller selves, that is, mind, body and spirit (Kakir, 1990).

While this cultural predisposition towards the scientific may have led to some revolutionary technological advances, there is a real danger in extending this approach when trying to do business with people whose ways of seeing the world are very different.

As the American scholar Alfred Shutz pointed out:

'When we encounter other social systems they have *already* given names to themselves, decided how they want to live and how the world is to be interpreted. We may label them if we wish but we cannot expect them to understand or accept our definitions, unless these correspond to their own. We cannot strip people of their common sense constructs or routine ways of seeing. They come to us as whole systems of patterned meanings and understandings. We can only try to understand, and to do so means *starting* with the way they think, and building from there.' (Schutz, 1970)

People within organizations do not simply react to their environment as a ship might to waves. They actively select, interpret and create their environments. Most international business people have experienced the significance of this, for example when a head office tries to impose a programme or policy that does not 'fit' locally. The subtle forces of culture go to work, biting at its roots until it proves ineffective, or until management turn their attention to other matters.

Morality is a movable feast

The ways in which different groups of people interpret their environments and organize their activities are based on their specific cultural values and assumptions. Values are not objective things that have qualities like shape or colour. They are relational; they are values *for* someone and are embedded in particular social contexts and relationships. To take a simple example, because certain pastoral peoples of Africa attach such a high value to cattle economically and symbolically, they can distinguish hundreds of kinds of cattle and have names for them all. Similarly, the French have a highly elaborate language for varieties of cheese. Distinctions are made in some cultures which are not made, or are made differently, in others. Cultural beliefs and values include assumptions about what is good or bad, right or wrong. These are often implicit assumptions, taken for granted and often not explicitly elaborated. There may not be a separate word or expression for 'right', or it may be a very complex concept such as the German '*Recht*', which is morally loaded and can mean law, a legal or moral right, the ability to do something, correct, proper, and so on. The existence of a concept is critical for the types of questions that can be raised. Where notions or concepts are available, they provide a clue about a culture's styles of reasoning and ways of thinking about the world.

The anthropologist and Greek scholar Gregory Lloyd traced some of the differences between ancient Greek and Chinese political thought. He found that while Greek political debate was often of no more than theoretical interest with no practical consequences for the actual conduct of politics, the Chinese preoccupation, in theory and practice, was with the orderly and efficient running of the state. There was no discourse about ethics, about the ulimate nature of right and wrong (Lloyd, 1990). So members of different cultures may see the world they live in very differently. And it is not just a matter of reaching different conclusions about the world from the 'same' evidence; the very evidence which is given to them as members of different cultures – the very ways in which they represent to themselves the physical, social and moral universe they live in – may be different (Beattie, 1964). The practice of teaching or articulating a category of ideas called 'ethics' or morality in business or other professions, then, is probably bizarre to people in many other cultures. What you should do may be taken for granted and may not correspond with other people's assumptions about 'right' and 'wrong'.

Certain values often thought to be universal really do differ from culture to culture. What constitutes an ethical business practice is not the same everywhere. This can be an enormously difficult area in managing across cultures, as Hari Bedi noted (Bedi, 1991).

> Several managers at the Asian regional office of a European multinational debated what to do about their agent in Indonesia. Though successful, the agent was continually offering kick-backs to his customers and they considered this highly unacceptable behaviour. Without discussion with the agent, the European managers were preparing this ultimatum: either he stopped offering kick-backs or he would be fired.
>
> From the perspective of the Indonesian agent, however, there was nothing wrong with his behaviour. It was the company's actions he saw as corrupt. They were overtly maximizing offshore profit by maintaining artificially high transfer prices on the books. This action, accorded corporate respectability, the Indonesian manager found reprehensible because it deprived Indonesia of its due share of taxes.

Both parties held certain assumptions about business practices they considered 'right' or 'moral'. Their beliefs were based on the particular cultures they came from and each thought their own beliefs were correct.

Perceptions of other cultures: USA–Europe

Understandably, people tend to notice what is surprising to them rather than what is the same. So every culture tends to form stereotypes of other cultures, usually based on exaggerated forms of behaviour. Even those who are very experienced in another culture can have expectations which turn out to be totally out of line when it comes to living in them.

Michael Johnson is an American editor who has spent most of his life abroad, including several years in Paris and in Moscow well before *perestroika*. He is married to a French woman, speaks fluent French, and regularly takes his annual leave on the Atlantic coast of France. Such a person ought to be as well prepared as any to take on a managerial job for a French company in Paris. The result is reported in Box 1.3.

Box 1.3   An American executive in Paris

'When I took a job with a French company, I was to be the first in a *nouvelle vogue* of foreigners who would bring Anglo-Saxon rigour to the operation and also help it develop its international ambitions. As I began applying tried-and-true Anglo-Saxon management techniques, I gradually realized that we had not understood each other. The French did not know what Anglo-Saxony is all about, and I did not expect the company's culture to be so resistant to change.

'Before leaving London, I asked friends for advice on how to adapt to the new rules I knew I would face. "Praise them for everything they do well – watch for the good work", one cross-cultural consultant urged. "People crave approval in every culture." Another predicted that the time was right – France was leading the way into a federated Europe, and a bit of cultural mixing could only be welcomed. Still another told me to stop worrying – my own curiosity and affection for the country would shine through.

'All of them were wrong. However well-advised one is, however pro-French one starts out, it probably will be a shock to peel back the layers of the true work culture and see what lies beneath. Even experienced Euromanagers, the hardened veterans of the international job circuit, are pulled up short by some of the contentious conduct in the workplace in France. Trust does not come easily to the French. Relations with most colleagues are suspicious, wary, watchful. Only among family and long-standing friendships, preferably dating back to childhood, are these hesitations overcome.

'At least a pinch of trust and good faith must be present in productive work relationships. Sharing of tasks certainly cannot be undertaken without it. A foreigner managing a French team will quickly yearn for this missing element as he tries to build a working machine.

'As I established my weekly meeting routine, I always began by citing work well done. But a senior member of the staff sniffed to the assembled team, "He only wants to give us good news." So much for the value of praise. Support from the top was assumed to be suspect. What might management want next? Our lives? I soon switched tactics, only to find that criticism went down even worse – raising hackles, and touching off defensive retorts.

'From the outside, it takes a while to realize that the very concept of management in many French companies is different. The British or American manager sees his role as a coordinator of resources and activities. He judges it useless or even harmful to be more competent than his subordinates in their own activities. Each member of the team is invited to contribute a separate skill or expertise, making the combination more than the sum of its parts.

continues

continued

'The French executive, in contrast, considers it important to have precise answers to any questions that subordinates might have about the work they are doing. "Implicitly, he bases his authority more on a superior degree of knowledge and competence than on his talent for coordination and management", says one academic study. The French manager does everything better, most of all giving sharply defined orders. The result, in a word, is centralization in France, and decentralization in the USA. The scene is thus set for basic misapprehensions.

'Early in my tenure, the French government's computer company with the wonderful name of Groupe Bull fell to squabbling in public with the industry minister who was responsible for the billion-dollar annual subsidy needed to keep Bull afloat. It looked like time for a reality check at Groupe Bull. At my weekly staff meeting I enthused over the journalistic opportunity this presented. Our reporting team would expose the nature of the fight, find out whether this was to be the last agony of Bull, and reveal whatever future plans for saving, merging or dissolving Bull were likely to be implemented. To achieve this considerable task in a week, I named a project coordinator and asked everyone on the staff to contribute.

'"You have all been in this business a long time," I reminded them. "You must all have friends and contacts inside Bull. Get on the phone." Another of the heavy silences I was getting used to then settled over the conference table. But I chirped on about the fun we were going to have getting to grips with this story. I then withdrew, and waited for the result.

'When the story was produced a week later, I realized no one had grasped what I was talking about. Most of the story had been reported and written by the man assigned to coordinate it. A few crumbs were contributed by one or two others. The collaborative effort I had ordered simply did not happen. The concept of teamwork was alien to the culture. Was there a lack of trust that each contributor would some-how benefit? Was there a suspicion that collaborative work was anti-individualistic? I swallowed hard and admitted to myself that teaming up on projects was not going to happen with a wave of my management wand. I had been so far off target that I couldn't find the words to express my frustration. It was perhaps a mistake not to have legislated teamwork then and there. Or would that have made for even less collaborative spirit? For the first time, my French vocabulary failed me and we simply blundered further into the unknown.

'In less than two years, I was back in London and the company had turned inward again. The chairman has since told associates he has no plans for international growth.'

Michael Johnson's experiences were traumatic for him and for his family. Yet how many people could be expected to be more successful than he? You can imagine similar frustrations and disbelief from a French manager trying to apply his or her managerial assumptions in an individualistic, entrepreneurial North American environment.

In international business, it is especially important to realize that seemingly 'neutral' behaviours can generate very different perceptions by the people experiencing them. Table 1.1 shows some very generalized behaviours of Americans and Europeans and then describes how each interprets that behaviour. The table gives only generalized perceptions of and by each side showing that the assumptions behind one person's behaviour are not necessarily shared by people from other cultures. The basis of these perceptions will be explored in the following chapter.

Differences even among neighbours

Great cultural diversity exists even between cultures in close proximity such as those within Europe, between Canada, the USA and Mexico, and between Japan and Singapore. And arguably regional differences within countries are just as significant as the arbitrarily drawn boundaries of nations. Their assumptions about doing business – planning, leadership, negotiating, motivating and conducting meetings – differ. There are also differences in the ways they tend to express themselves and in the importance of family, work, material success and other basic values.

Cultural consistency across Asia/Pacific is almost non-existent too: in terms of development levels, the spectrum runs from one of the world's richest countries, Japan, to several of the poorest. Some countries have high definition TV, while in others a phone call is a luxury. The range of political structures is equally daunting to the searchers for universality, taking them from the consensus-seeking democratic sophistication of Japan to the many and varied faces of totalitarianism. As is true in Europe, Asia/Pacific contains a plethora of languages (within as well as between countries), all the world's major religions and several ethnic types. The only common denominator in the region is that of being non-Western – and even that is inconsistently spread by the extensive borrowing, or imposition of widely differing Western ideas, ideals, techniques and systems over the past centuries (Redding and Baldwin, 1991).

Creating a global organization out of diversity

So what do all these differences mean to organizations trying to operate globally? There is no shortage of books and consultancy reports on the necessity and process of becoming global. Indeed, the new terminology includes the idea of developing a 'network' that holds the whole thing together. This idea will be explored in Chapter 3, but essentially managers are being told that, to be global, it is necessary to have a shared set of values in the organization. Kenichi Ohmae, managing director of McKinsey & Co. in Japan, describes in his book *The Borderless World* how in a global organization 'before national identity, before local affiliation, before German ego or Italian ego or Japanese ego – before any of this comes the commitment to a single, unified global mission'. Furthermore, he writes that to be global 'you really have to believe, deep down, that people may work "in" different national environments but are not "of" them. What they are "of" is the global corporation.' He acknowledges that managing the network that holds together such an organization is 'inherently messy' (Ohmae, 1990).

The question left for those who are charged with creating and managing this 'amoeba-like' network is: how is it possible for an organization operating across cultures to manage the 'mess' of cultural diversity and still maintain a sense of being integrated, with a common purpose and corporate culture? As with the computer company described above that issued its misunderstood '11 Operating Principles' worldwide, maintaining a shared set of values is no simple task, if indeed it is even possible. Chapter 5 attempts to shed some light on how some companies moving in this direction are actually managing the meaning of their organizations across cultures.

The competitive advantage of culture

To begin to think about cultural differences as a source of competitive advantage, there must be a shift in assumptions about the impact of cultural differences on global organizations. Culture should not simply be considered as an obstacle to doing business across cultures. It can provide tangible benefits and can be used competitively. As with individuals, nations have developed particular competencies, skills and ways of working, in areas that they value and that make sense in their environment. At the same time, as with individuals, they lose competencies in

Table 1.1   European and American cultural behaviours: how we perceive each other.

American behaviour	Americans see own behaviour as	Europeans see American behaviour as	European behaviour	Europeans see own behaviour as	Americans see European behaviour as
Trust more	Constructive	Naïve childishness	Trust less	Realism	Cynicism, nihilism
Make many friends	Friendly, open	Superficial, insincere	Have fewer close friends	Discretion, depth	Cold, distant
Smooth differences	Cooperative, democratic, practical	Lack conviction, depth	Dispute differences	Refining the truth through dialectic	Argumentative, implacable, irreconcilable
Collaborate easily	Others will join you if it is in their common interest. Common interests dominate, conspiracies are evil	Containing hidden agendas	Collaborate cautiously	Others will block you. Conflicting, territorial interests, conspiracies are normal	Distrustful of each other
Be optimistic and express optimism	Life is rich	Foolishness	Be cautious, express reservations	Resources limited	Pessimistic, masochistic
Seek opportunity	The right time is now	Aggressiveness	Act out of purpose	The right time will show itself	Out of touch
Mix business and pleasure	Life is a continuum	Never stop doing business, workaholics	Separate business and private life	Everything has its time and place	Compartmentalized, schizophrenic
Think out loud, brainstorm	The more ideas, the better the product or solution	Scatterbrained, undisciplined	Prepare what you say	Be accountable for your words	Cautious, guarded, lacking spontaneity
Behave spontaneously	Free, creative	Irresponsible, immature	Behave logically, rationally	Mature, responsible	Staid, stilted, repressed
Decentralized politics	People can solve their own problems	Chaotic, unreliable	Centralized politics	Controls and limits, ensure everyone is cared for	Bureaucratic and dictorial tendencies
Do it, theorize later	Being practical	Rationalization, error prone	Theory before action	Doing it right	Impractical, idealist, action is often too late

Table 1.1   *continued*

American behaviour	Americans see own behaviour as	Europeans see American behaviour as	European behaviour	Europeans see own behaviour as	Americans see European behaviour as
Create open information flow	Enabling the relationship	No substance	Guarded information flow, indirection	Enabling the relationship	Secretive
Take pride in accomplishment	You become someone through doing things	Petit bourgeois	Take pride in yourself and your group	Maintain dignity by living out your calling	Vanity without substance
Attack because of the result	Getting things done is what counts	Unprincipled, small-minded	Attack because of the process	Correctness and style are paramount	Uncommitted to results
Base authority and hierarchy on accomplishment	Positions exist while they are practical and functional	Poor judges of character	Accept hierarcy as based in the nature of things	Position is based on the kind of person. *Noblesse oblige*	Autocratic, non-democratic
Avoid differentiating female and male roles	Trying to be more fair and egalitarian	Debasing both women and men	Differentiate male and female roles	Both men's and women's roles have their own prestige	Sexist, preserving outmoded traditions
Treat children as adults	Making choices helps them grow up	Children are loud and intrusive, delinquent	Discipline children	Discipline creates character	Severe, creates rebellion
Put freedom and initiative first	Respecting the individual	Socially irresponsible	Put duty and obedience first	Respecting the common good	Blind obedience, prone to dictatorship
Forgive mistakes	Trying is what counts – you will get there	Over-reaching themselves, imposters	Avoid mistakes	Mistakes are often irreparable	Over-cautious, miss opportunities, CYA (covering your backside)
Consume	Being alive, moving, spirit filled	Wastefulness, quantity over quality, meaninglessness	Be frugal	Strive for quality, not quantity	Smallness, meanness, obsessed with things not people
Civil violence	Personal or moral failure	Lawless, undisciplined culture	Political violence	Conflict of group interest	Innate contentiousness and hatred for others

Source: Dr George Simmons, author of *Transcultural Leadership*, created the chart from a study done by Stuart Miller (*Understanding Europeans* (1990). John Muir Press), other publications and his own experience as an international management consultant.

areas that they do not value. In turn they can put greater value on the things they are good at and value less the things they are not good at, reinforcing their particular competencies. In consequence nations, and to some extent different regions or sub-nations, can offer unique competencies to global organizations. Michael Porter has explored these interactions extensively in his book *The Competitive Advantage of Nations* (Porter, 1990). Cultural advantages can arise from differing values and ways of seeing the world. To realize competitive advantage from them, it is first necessary to try to understand them. However, only a few organizations are beginning to do this.

Case 1.1   Using culture competitively at ICI

ICI (Imperial Chemical Industries), the world's 38th largest industrial corporation, has been making big strides in its efforts to internationalize. Since the early 1980s, the British concern has reorganized into worldwide business units, a number of which have their headquarters outside the UK. To develop a more global perspective, it changed the composition of the 16-person board of directors from being all-British to include several non-British executives (currently a German, a Canadian and two Americans). In addition to integrating different cultural perspectives at the top, ICI is finding ways to use culture competitively at a deeper level in the organization.

One recent cultural initiative at ICI involved a group of Italian and British managers from ICI Pharma Italy and their counterparts from ICI Pharmaceuticals headquarters in Cheshire, in the UK. In recent years, the Italian operation has been playing an increasingly important role within the business unit internationally. However, when working on joint projects, the British and Italian managers often found communication difficult and frustrating, even though they all spoke English. The group decided it was important and necessary to understand better each other's ways of doing things, so they undertook an exercise they called 'Project Management in a Multi-Cultural Environment'.

With the help of consultants, the two teams identified the areas where they were experiencing real difficulties in working together and openly shared the perceptions each had of the other culture. The differences in focus and process to get things done are summarized in general terms below.

continues

continued

Differences between British and Italian working attitudes

UK	versus	*Italy*
'Doing things the right way'	versus	'Doing the right things'
Working to protocols and standards	versus	Encouraging flexibility
Establishing procedures to get things done	versus	Building relationships to get things done
Providing essential information	versus	Providing context
Diplomacy	versus	Directness in communication

The British managers depicted the Italian business culture as:

A fluid, relatively unstructured organization. Seen from a positive perspective, Italian managers are resourceful improvisers who are able to adjust to changes, to circumvent constraints and to adapt to, or create, new rules for the game. More negatively, the image of the Italian manager is one of an excessively flexible, ever-changing, time-unconscious Mediterranean who has to be checked and double-checked all the time if you want to be sure that agreed objectives are realized.

British perceptions of Italians

- Excessively flexible
- Entrepreneurs
- Creative
- Rely on people, not structures
- Emotional
- Undisciplined
- Never meet deadlines
- Not very time-conscious
- Aversion to planning

The Italian managers characterized the British business culture as:

Having a penchant for tradition, a narrow definition of responsibility, and a high level of concern for form and order. The British are well-organized, analytical thinkers, very much preoccupied with rules and procedures. That something is 'simply not done' is a frequently heard phrase. On the one hand, this could be positive. On the other hand, it means that the British adhere to a management style that works against innovation and change. The emphasis on protocol and procedures gives them a reputation for being 'inelastic', too process-oriented and sometimes slow and ponderous.

continues

continued

Italian perceptions of the British

- Obsessed with rules and procedures
- Inflexible
- Formal
- Avoid confrontation
- Inhibited/hide emotions
- Disciplined
- Good planners
- Suspicious
- Slow and ponderous

In the process of making explicit their perceptions about each other, the teams recognized that both cultures' behaviours were perfectly legitimate and professional in their respective environments. In fact, the perceptions of each other were precisely those things that made each successful in their own environment. The Italian flexibility in business that was so often a source of frustration to the British managers was a valued and important quality for success in Italy. The formality and relative structure that frustrated Italian managers would be inappropriate in the Italian business environment but made sense in the UK. One Italian manager explained:

'We, from ICI Pharma Italy, operate and plan in compliance with our rapidly moving environment. It requires periodic adaptations to new and changing situations. Obviously, this has its repercussions on, for example, the implementation of medium- and long-term planning. Our Italian business environment requires us to struggle every day against turbulence, and therefore we need a flexible attitude. Operating according to the British methods and conventions can lead to a loss of opportunities. Worse, we would be dead in a few months!'

Both groups of managers recognized that neither culture was right or wrong. They simply used opposite starting points of the same logic.

Instead of considering their cultural differences as distinct, incompatible ways of viewing the world, they worked out particular ways of integrating the strengths of each within the context of management. Most importantly, this included valuing what each approach had to offer. Also, they decided that they could identify particular aspects of joint projects in which one or the other approach would be more appropriate. These efforts are continuing because the teams recognize that it is a process that must be worked on over time, but benefits are already being realized. One year after the workshop, participants met again to celebrate the successful completion on time of a key phase in an important project. Both groups believe that they have made real gains in being able to use each other's strengths more effectively and, over time, using them to build competitive advantage.

Summary

Culture is about the way people understand their world and make sense of it. It is only when these taken for granted assumptions are challenged that people realize that they even exist. It is very much like the story of the boy who announced that the emperor was naked, when both the emperor and all his other subjects perceived his dress to be magnificent.

Business and politics are not discrete, rational domains of activity separate from a society's particular cultural beliefs and values. All social behaviour is embedded in a particular context and is connected to other deeply held values and beliefs. This means that the stakes are high for mismanaging cultural differences. Ignoring or mishandling differences can mean inability to retain and motivate employees, misreading the potential of cross-border alliances, marketing and advertising blunders, and failure to build sustainable sources of competitive advantage. Mismanaging cultural differences can render otherwise successful managers and organizations ineffective and frustrated when working across cultures. When successfully managed, however, differences in culture can lead to innovative business practices, faster and better learning within the organization, and sustainable sources of competitive advantage.

To begin to think about cultural differences as a source of competitive advantage, there must be a shift in assumptions about the impact of cultural differences on global organizations. Culture should not simply be considered as an obstacle to doing business across cultures. It can provide tangible benefits and can be used competitively. While there are no clear-cut or universal 'answers' on how to manage cultural differences for each business area of this book, for all of the reasons outlined in this chapter, it is possible to explore the impact of culture on each area and provide frameworks for considering cultural factors. By learning something about the variety of human cultures, and about how that variety affects people's approach to business, it is possible to see that your own solutions may not be the only, the best or the most appropriate for the task at hand. It is this basic realization that is the first step in using cultural differences strategically.

References

Beattie J. (1964). *Other Cultures: Aims, Methods and Achievements in Social Anthropology.* London: Routledge

Bedi H. (1991). *Understanding the Asian Manager*, pp. 37–38. Sydney, Australia: Allen & Unwin

Doktor R.H. (1990). Asian and American CEOs: a comparative study. *Organizational Dynamics*, **18**(3) p. 49

Hampden-Turner C. and Trompenaars F. (1993). *The Seven Cultures of Capitalism: Value Systems for Creating Wealth in the United States, Britain, Japan, Germany, France, Sweden, and the Netherlands*. New York: Doubleday

Institutional Investor (1991). Insurance companies with worldly ambitions. 30 January

Kakir (1990). In Tambiah S.J. *Magic, Science, Religion and the Scope of Rationality*, pp. 99–101. Cambridge: Cambridge University Press

Laurent A. (1983). The cultural diversity of Western conceptions of management. *International Studies of Management and Organization*, **XIII**(1–2), Spring-Summer, 1983, pp. 75–96

Lloyd G.E.R. (1990). *Demystifying Mentalities*. Cambridge: Cambridge University Press

Manchau W. (1991). UK: Performance at CMB Packaging highlights problems of Anglo-French mergers. *The Times*, 11 September

Miller D. (1993). *Unwrapping Christmas*. Oxford: Clarendon Press

Nagashima N. (1973). A Reversed World: Or Is It? The Japanese Way of Communicating and Their Attitudes Towards Alien Cultures. In Horton and Finnegan R. *Modes of Thought*. London: Faber and Faber

Ohmae K. (1990). *The Borderless World: Power and Strategy in the Interlinked Economy*, p.96. London: Collins

Porter M. E. (1990). *The Competitive Advantage of Nations*. New York: The Free Press

Redding G. (1992). The comparative management theory zoo; getting the elephants and ostriches and even dinosaurs from the jungle into the iron cages. Paper presented at the Conference *Perspectives on International Business: Theory, Research and Institutional Arrangements*, University of South Carolina, May 1992, pp. 5–11

Redding S.G. and Baldwin E. (1991). *Managers for Asia/Pacific: Recruitment and Development Strategies*, p.20. London: the Economist Intelligence Unit

Schutz A. (1970). *Phenomenology and Social Relations*. (Wagner, R. ed.). Chicago: University of Chicago Press

Smith P.B. and Bond M.H. (1993). *Social Psychology Across Cultures: Analysis and Perspectives*. London: Harvester Wheatsheaf

Trompenaars F. (1993). *Riding the Waves of Culture*. London: The Economist Books

Wall Street Journal, (1990). August

Winch P. (1970). Understanding a Primitive Society. In Wilson B., *Rationality*. Oxford: Basil Blackwell Press

2

Culture: what it is, what it is not and how it directs organizational behaviour

Most people who have visited or worked in another country would read-ily agree that cultural differences exist. They might point to such things as different styles of dress, language, food or mannerisms as examples of how cultures differ. It is much more difficult to go beyond such relevant, yet superficial differences in talking about culture. If you are fluent in another language, some of the more 'hidden' differences become more apparent, such as how and when people use humour, how formally or informally they behave towards others in different contexts, and the different meanings and use of silence, power, influence, gender, position, and so on. But these are most often noticed in a particular situation, labelled as 'strange' or different and then disregarded because we have no way of classifying these peculiarities into a 'language of culture'. Because culture is about pervasive, deeply held and implicit beliefs and values, it is indeed difficult to find a language with which to discuss it or to explore its consequences.

'It is helpful… to think of culture as analogous to music: (a) If another person hasn't heard a particular piece of music, it is impossible to describe. (b) Before the days of written scores, people had to learn informally by imitation. (c) People were able to exploit the potential of music only when they started writing musical scores.' (Hall, 1973)

The difficulty of finding terms with which to explore differences in culture does not seem to stop people from talking about culture as if it were a 'thing', hovering over a society and influencing behaviour in a direct and uniform way. At the end of 1990 when Renault of France lost out on the Skoda deal to Volkswagen of Germany, the international press reported that Renault blamed its failure on culture (*International Herald Tribune*, 1990). They seemed to think that Germany had a culture closer to the Czech culture than did France. The validity of the claim is not the issue here. The point is that the perception of culture as the determinant of such an important outcome is so readily offered (and, it could be added, accepted) as an explanation when most people would have a difficult time being specific about *what that might really mean* except in terms of the superficial examples given above. Culture is not a 'thing' which can be experienced directly through the senses, just as 'needs', 'social systems', 'evil' and 'peace' are not directly tangible or visible. They are ideas constructed from within a society. 'Culture' does not exist in a simple and easily defined form for a specifiable number of people in a bounded area. And, obviously, a society does not consist of individuals with entirely uniform mental characteristics or personalities.

What culture is

(1) *A shared system of meanings.* Culture dictates what groups of people pay attention to. It guides how the world is perceived, how the self is experienced and how life itself is organized. Individuals of a group share patterns that enable them to see the same things in the same way and this holds them together. Each person carries within them learned ways of finding meaning in their experiences. In order for effective, stable and meaningful interaction to occur, people must have a shared system of meaning. There must be some common ways of understanding events and behaviour, and ways of anticipating how other people in your social group are likely to behave. For example, waving a hand or planting a kiss has no clear meaning without the context being understood. Furthermore, the intended meaning of a gesture need not coincide with the perceived meaning except where cultural identities match. It is only when the meanings *do* coincide that effective communication can happen.

(2) *Relative.* There is no cultural absolute. People in different cultures perceive the world differently and have different ways of doing things, and there is no set standard for considering one group as intrinsically superior or inferior to any other. Each national culture is relative to other cultures' ways of perceiving the world and doing things.

(3) *Learned.* Culture is derived from your social environment, not from your genetic make-up.
(4) *About groups.* Culture is a collective phenomenon that is about shared values and meanings.

The noted business author and scholar Geert Hofstede describes culture as the 'collective programming of the mind' and explains that it lies between human nature on one side and individual personality on the other (Hofstede, 1991). Figure 2.1 shows his model of three levels of uniqueness in human mental programming.

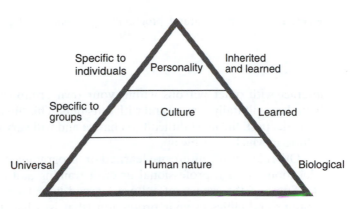

Figure 2.1 Three levels of human mental programming. (*Source*: Adapted from Hofstede, 1991)

What culture is not

(1) *Right or wrong.*
(2) *Inherited.*
(3) *About individual behaviour.* There are wide variations in individual values and behaviour within each national culture.

Different layers of culture

Each person carries around several layers of cultural 'programming'. It starts when a child learns basic values: what is right and wrong, good and bad, logical and illogical, beautiful and ugly. Culture is about your fundamental assumptions of what it is to be a person and how you should

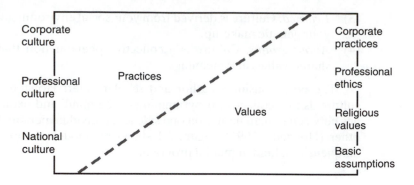

Figure 2.2   Layers of cultural 'programming'. (*Source*: Adapted from Hofstede, 1991)

interact with other persons within your own group (which again is a boundary culturally drawn) and with outsiders. This 'first level' of culture is the deepest, the most difficult to change and will vary according to the culture in which we grow up.

Other layers of culture are learned or 'programmed' in the course of education, through professional or craft training and in organizational life. Some of the aspects of culture learned later have to do with conventions and ethics in your profession (that is, what it means to be a lawyer, accountant or doctor; the way a particular organization functions, how people get promoted or how office politics are played, and so on). These layers are more ways of doing things, or *practices*, as opposed to fundamental assumptions about how things are (see Figure 2.2).

Because of the timing and sequence of learning these values and ways of doing things, their capacity for change is also different. André Laurent uses the diagram shown in Figure 2.3 to illustrate change capability (Laurent, 1989). Individuals and societies have a lower capability for change than do organizations.

Cultural values taken for granted

Cultural values are very difficult to talk about because they are taken for granted. They become like a problem solved regularly in the same way: it ceases to be a problem. Rather, it ceases to be a conscious act and becomes just another assumption. It is only when a person's assumptions are challenged that they realize that these assumptions even exist.

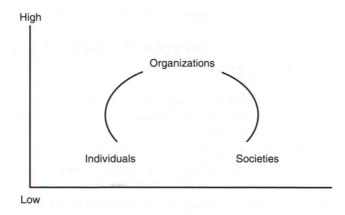

Figure 2.3 Change capability. (*Source*: Evans, Doz, and Laurent, eds., 1989)

Definitions of culture

There are many descriptions and definitions of culture (see Box 2.1).

Attempts to classify national cultures in terms of the importance attached to different values

The most widely known research in the attempt to compare national cultures in terms of broad value differences is the pioneering work of Geert Hofstede. From his research with a very large sample of employees from 50 countries and three regions within a single organization, IBM, Hofstede identified four dimensions of work-related value differences. These are power distance, uncertainty avoidance, individualism/collectivism and masculinity/femininity. Values, according to Hofstede's definition, are 'a broad tendency to prefer certain states of affairs over others'. These differences in preferences, or values, have important implications for managers and organizations operating across cultural borders. He describes the dimensions as follows (Hofstede, 1991). (Box 2.2 gives some of the most useful questions and responses in defining the meanings of each of these dimensions.)

Box 2.1   Concepts of culture by some of the gurus

Tylor E. (1871). That complex whole which includes knowledge, beliefs, art, morals, laws, customs and any other capabilities and habits acquired by man as a member of society.

Herskovits M.J. (1948). The man-made part of the human environment.

Kroeber A.L. and Kluckhohn C. (1952). Transmitted patterns of values, ideas and other symbolic systems that shape behaviour.

Becker and Geer (1970). Set of common understandings expressed in language.

van Maanen J. and Schein E.H. (1979). Values, beliefs and expectations that members come to share.

Schwartz M.C. and Jordon D.K. (1980). Pattern of beliefs and expectations shared by members that produce norms shaping behaviour.

Hofstede G.H. (1980). The collective programming of the mind which distinguishes the members of one human group from another.

Louis M.R. (1983). Three aspects: (1) some content (meaning and interpretation) (2) peculiar to (3) a group.

Hall E.T. and Hall M.R. (1987). Primarily a system for creating, sending, storing and processing information.

Harris P.R. and Moran R.T. (1987). A distinctly human capacity for adapting to circumstances and transmitting this coping skill and knowledge to subsequent generations.

Power distance

Power distance is the extent to which inequality (a pecking order or hierarchy) is seen as an irreducible fact of life. It would condition the extent to which employees accept that their boss has more power than they have and the extent to which they accept that their boss's opinions and decisions are right *because* he or she is the boss. A low power distance organizational setting is one where employees accept that their boss has more power and is right only when he or she knows the best way to do something and knows the correct answers. A report in a British newspaper described some of the different conceptions of power distance when British Petroleum attempted to mix 40 workers from 13 nations in a modern European finance office (*The Independent*, 1991).

Box 2.2 Hofstede's four dimensions of culture-related values

Value	Questionnaire item	Response
Power distance	How frequently, in your experience, does the following problem occur: employees being afraid to express their disagreement with their managers?	Frequently
Uncertainty avoidance	Company rules should not be broken, even if the employee thinks it is in the company's best interest.	Strongly agree
	How long do you think you will continue working for this company?	Until I retire
Individualism	How important is it to you to have a job which leaves you sufficient time for your personal or family life?	Very
	How important is it to you to have considerable freedom to adapt your own approach to the job?	Very
Femininity	How important is it to you to have a good working relationship with your manager?	Very
	How important is it to you to work with people who cooperate well with one another?	Very
Masculinity	How important is it to you to have an opportunity for high earnings?	Very
	How important is it to you to get the recognition you deserve when you do a good job?	Very

(*Source*: Smith P.B. and Bond M.H. *Social Psychology Across Cultures: Analysis and Perspectives*, p.39. London: Harvester Wheatsheaf)

The article reported that: 'Germans felt more comfortable in formal hierarchies, while Dutch members had a relaxed approach to authority. UK, Scandinavian and Dutch managers all expected their decision-making to be challenged, while French managers thought that authority to make decisions came as a right of office.'

In the larger power distance cultures superiors and subordinates consider each other as unequal; the hierarchical system is felt to be based on some existential inequality. Indigenous organizations centralize power more and subordinates are expected to be told what to do. Superiors are believed to be entitled to privileges in a high power distance culture. There are more visible signs of status, and contacts between superiors and subordinates are supposed to be initiated only by superiors.

In smaller power distance situations subordinates and superiors consider each other as more equal; the hierarchical system is just an inequality of roles, established for convenience and which may change depending on the circumstances. Organizations have a tendency to become decentralized, with flatter hierarchies and a limited number of supervisory personnel. Privileges for the top ranks are essentially undesirable, and superiors are expected to be accessible to subordinates. Organizations more often have in place ways of dealing with employee complaints about alleged power abuse (Adler, 1986).

Table 2.1   Power distance (PD) scores.

Score rank	Country or region	PD score	Score rank	Country or region	PD score
1	Malaysia	104	27/28	South Korea	60
2/3	Guatemala	95	29/30	Iran	58
2/3	Panama	95	29/30	Taiwan	58
4	Philippines	94	31	Spain	57
5/6	Mexico	81	32	Pakistan	55
5/6	Venezuela	81	33	Japan	54
7	Arab countries	80	34	Italy	50
8/9	Equador	78	35/36	Argentina	49
8/9	Indonesia	78	35/36	South Africa	49
10/11	India	77	37	Jamaica	45
10/11	West Africa	77	38	USA	40
12	Yugoslavia	76	39	Canada	39
13	Singapore	74	40	Netherlands	38
14	Brazil	69	41	Australia	36
15/16	France	68	42/44	Costa Rica	35
15/16	Hong Kong	68	42/44	West Germany	35
17	Colombia	67	42/44	UK	35
18/19	Salvador	66	45	Switzerland	34
18/19	Turkey	66	46	Finland	33
20	Belgium	65	47/48	Norway	31
21/23	East Africa	64	47/48	Sweden	31
21/23	Peru	64	49	Ireland (Republic of)	28
21/23	Thailand	64			
24/25	Chile	63	50	New Zealand	22
24/25	Portugal	63	51	Denmark	18
26	Uruguay	61	52	Israel	13
27/28	Greece	60	53	Austria	11

Table 2.2   Business areas affected by power distance.

Low power distance	High power distance
Less centralization	Greater centralization
Flatter organization pyramids	Steep organization pyramids
Managers seen as making decisions after consulting with subordinates	Managers seen as making decisions autocratically and paternalistically
Close supervision negatively evaluated by subordinates	Close supervision positively evaluated by subordinates
Managers like to see themselves as practical and systematic; they admit a need for support	Managers like to see themselves as benevolent decision-makers
Higher-educated employees hold much less authoritarian values than lower-educated ones	Higher- and lower-educated employees hold similar values about authority

Source: Adapted from Hofstede G. (1984). *Culture's Consequences: International Differences in Work-Related Values*, abridged edn. Thousand Oaks, CA: Sage Publications Inc. Reproduced with permission of McGraw-Hill.

Uncertainty avoidance

Uncertainty avoidance is the lack of tolerance for ambiguity and the need for formal rules. This dimension measures the extent to which people in a society feel threatened by and try to avoid ambiguous situations. They may do this by establishing more formal rules, rejecting deviant ideas and behaviour, and accepting the possibility of absolute truths and the attainment of unchallengeable expertise.

Lifetime employment is more common in high uncertainty avoidance countries such as Japan, Portugal and Greece, whereas high job mobility more commonly occurs in low uncertainty avoidance countries such as Singapore, Hong Kong, Denmark and the USA (Adler, 1986).

Management implications of power distance and uncertainty avoidance

These two dimensions, power distance and uncertainty avoidance, affect our thinking about organizations. In addition to the affected business areas listed in Tables 2.2 and 2.4, taking these two dimensions together reveals differences in the implicit model people from different cultures may have about organizational structure and functioning. Organizing demands answers to two important questions:

(1)   Who has the power to decide what?
(2)   What rules or procedures will be followed to attain the desired ends?

Table 2.3 Uncertainty avoidance (UA) scores.

Score rank	Country or region	UA score	Score rank	Country or region	UA score
1	Greece	112	28	Equador	67
2	Portugal	104	29	West Germany	65
3	Guatemala	101	30	Thailand	64
4	Uruguay	100	31/32	Iran	59
5/6	Belgium	94	31/32	Finland	59
5/6	Salvador	94	33	Switzerland	58
7	Japan	92	34	West Africa	54
8	Yugoslavia	88	35	Netherlands	53
9	Peru	87	36	East Africa	52
10/15	France	86	37	Australia	51
10/15	Chile	86	38	Norway	50
10/15	Spain	86	39/40	South Africa	49
10/15	Costa Rica	86	39/40	New Zealand	49
10/15	Panama	86	41/42	Indonesia	48
10/15	Argentina	86	41/42	Canada	48
16/17	Turkey	85	43	USA	46
16/17	South Korea	85	44	Philippines	44
18	Mexico	82	45	India	40
19	Israel	81	46	Malaysia	36
20	Colombia	80	47/48	UK	35
21/22	Venezuela	76	47/48	Ireland	35
21/22	Brazil	76		(Republic of)	
23	Italy	75	49/50	Hong Kong	29
24/25	Pakistan	70	49/50	Sweden	29
24/25	Austria	70	51	Denmark	23
26	Taiwan	69	52	Jamaica	13
27	Arab countries	68	53	Singapore	8

Table 2.4 Business areas affected by uncertainty avoidance.

Low uncertainty avoidance	High uncertainty avoidance
Greater readiness to live by the day	More worry about the future
Less emotional resistance to change	More emotional resistance to change
Less hesitation to change employers	Tendency to stay with same employer
Loyalty to employer is not seen as a virtue	Loyalty to employer is seen as a virtue
Managers should be selected on other criteria than seniority	Managers should be selected on the basis of seniority
More risk-taking	Less risk-taking
Hope of success	Fear of failure
A manager need not be an expert in the field he or she manages	A manager must be an expert in the field he or she manages
Conflict in organizations is natural	Conflict in organizations is undesirable
Delegation to subordinates can be complete	Initiative of subordinates should be kept under control
Employee optimism about the motives behind company activities	Employee pessimism about the motives behind company activities
Rules may be broken for pragmatic reasons	Rules should not be broken

Source: Adapted from Hofstede G. (1984). *Culture's Consequences: International Differences in Work-Related Values*, abridged edn. Thousand Oaks, CA: Sage Publications Inc. Reproduced with permission of McGraw-Hill.

The answer to the first question is influenced by indigenous cultural norms of power distance; the answer to the second question by the cultural norms about uncertainty avoidance. Taken together these two dimensions reveal a remarkable contrast in a society's acceptance and conception of an organization and the mechanisms that are employed in controlling and coordinating activities within it (Hofstede, 1991).

Some researchers have tried to measure the link between the 'implicit' models of organization and objectively assessable characteristics of organizational structure. In the 1970s, Owen James Stevens, an American professor at INSEAD business school in France, presented his students with a case study exam which dealt with a conflict between two department heads within a company (Hofstede, 1991). His students consisted primarily of French, German and British students. In Figure 2.4 their countries are located in the lower right, lower left and upper left quadrants respectively. Stevens had noticed a difference in the way 200 students of different nationalities had handled the case in previous exams. The students had been required individually to come up with both their diagnosis of the problem and their suggested solution. Stevens sorted these exams by the nationality of the author and then compared the answers. The results were striking. The majority of French diagnosed the case as negligence by the general manager to whom the two department heads reported. The solution they preferred was for the opponents in the conflict to take the issue to their common boss, who would issue orders for settling such dilemmas in the future. Stevens interpreted the implicit organization model of the French as a 'pyramid of people': the general manager at the top of the pyramid, and each successive level at its proper place below.

The majority of the Germans diagnosed the case as a lack of structure. They tended to think that the competence of the two conflicting department heads had not been clearly specified. The solution they preferred was to establish specific procedures which could include calling in a consultant, nominating a task force, or asking the common boss. According to Stevens, the Germans saw the organization as a 'well-oiled machine' in which intervention by management should be limited because the rules should settle day-to-day problems.

The majority of the British diagnosed the case as a human relationships problem. They saw the two department heads as poor negotiators who would benefit from attending, preferably together, a management course to improve their skills. Stevens thought their implicit model of a 'village market' led them to look at the problem in terms of the demands of the situation determining what will happen, rather than hierarchy or rules.

A society's position on these two dimensions does seem to influence the implicit model of the organization in that society, and the kinds of coordination mechanisms that people in that culture would tend to rely upon.

Employees in high power distance and low uncertainty avoidance countries such as Singapore, Hong Kong and Indonesia tend to think of their organizations as traditional families. The patriarch, or head of the

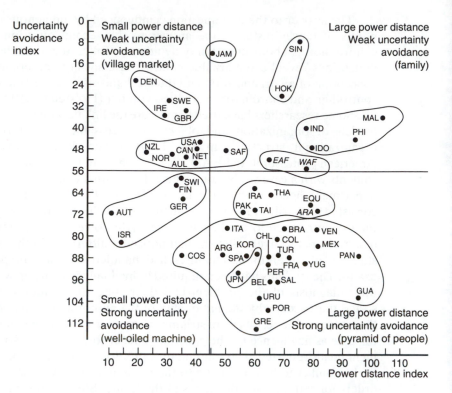

Figure 2.4 Power distance and uncertainty avoidance scores.

Key

ARA	Arab-speaking countries (Egypt, Lebanon, Lybia, Kuwait, Iraq, Saudi Arabia, United Arab Emirates)	FRA	France	PAK	Pakistan
		GBR	Great Britain	PAN	Panama
		GER	West Germany (formerly)	PER	Peru
				PHI	Philippines
		GRE	Greece	POR	Portugal
		GUA	Guatemala	SAF	South Africa
ARG	Argentina	HOK	Hong Kong	SAL	Salvador
AUL	Australia	IDO	Indonesia	SIN	Singapore
AUT	Austria	IND	India	SPA	Spain
BEL	Belgium	IRA	Iran	SWE	Sweden
BRA	Brazil	IRE	Ireland (Republic of)	TAI	Taiwan
CAN	Canada	ISR	Israel	THA	Thailand
CHL	Chile	ITA	Italy	TUR	Turkey
COL	Columbia	JAM	Jamaica	URU	Uruguay
COS	Costa Rica	JPN	Japan	USA	United States
DEN	Denmark	KOR	South Korea	VEN	Venezuela
EAF	East Africa (Kenya, Ethiopia, Tanzania, Zambia)	MAL	Malaysia	WAF	West Africa (Nigeria, Ghana, Sierra Leone)
		MEX	Mexico		
		NET	Netherlands		
EQA	Equador	NOR	Norway	YUG	Yugoslavia (formerly)
FIN	Finland	NZL	New Zealand		

family, is expected to protect family members physically and economically in exchange for unwavering loyalty from its members. The most likely coordination and control mechanism for the family is a standardization of work processes by specifying the contents of work – who does the chores.

Employees in countries such as France, Brazil, Portugal and Mexico that are high on both dimensions tend to view organizations as pyramids of people rather than as families. Everyone knows who reports to whom, and formal and activating lines of communication run vertically through the organization. Management reduces uncertainty and provides coordination and control by emphasizing who has authority over whom and in what way this authority can be exercised.

Where high uncertainty avoidance and low power distance are combined, in such countries as Israel, Austria, Germany and Switzerland, organizations are perceived as well-oiled machines; they are highly predictable without the imposition of a strong hierarchy. Uncertainty is reduced by clearly defining roles and procedures. Coordination and control are achieved primarily through standardization and certification of skills, specifying the training required to perform the work.

In cultures where there is low uncertainty avoidance and low power distance, the relevant organizational model is a 'village market'. Countries such as Denmark, Ireland, Norway, the UK and the USA are representative of this model. People will feel less comfortable with strict and formal rules or with what would be perceived as unnecessary layers of hierarchy. Control and coordination tends to take place through mutual adjustment of people through informal communication, and by specifying the desired results.

Individualism/collectivism

Individualism is a concern for yourself as an individual as opposed to concern for the priorities and rules of the group to which you belong. The majority of the people in the world live in societies where the interests of the group take precedence over the interests of the individual. In these societies, the group to which you belong is the major source of your identity and the unit to which you owe lifelong loyalty. For only a minority of the world's population do individual interests prevail over group interests. People in these cultures tend to think of themselves as 'I' and as distinct from other people's 'I's (Hofstede, 1984). People tend to classify themselves and each other by individual characteristics, rather than by group membership. Healthy people in individualistic societies are thought to be independent of others and able to 'stand on their own two feet'.

Table 2.5   Individualism (IDV) scores.

Score rank	Country or region	IDV score	Score rank	Country or region	IDV score
1	USA	91	26/27	Arab countries	38
2	Australia	90	28	Turkey	37
3	UK	89	29	Uruguay	36
4/5	Canada	80	30	Greece	35
4/5	Netherlands	80	31	Philippines	32
6	New Zealand	79	32	Mexico	30
7	Italy	76	33/35	East Africa	27
8	Belgium	75	33/35	Yugoslavia	27
9	Denmark	74	33/35	Portugal	27
10/11	Sweden	71	36	Malaysia	26
10/11	France	71	37	Hong Kong	25
12	Ireland (Republic of)	70	38	Chile	23
			39/41	West Africa	20
13	Norway	69	39/41	Singapore	20
14	Switzerland	68	39/41	Thailand	20
15	West Germany	67	42	Salvador	19
16	South Africa	65	43	South Korea	18
17	Finland	63	44	Taiwan	17
18	Austria	55	45	Peru	16
19	Israel	54	46	Costa Rica	15
20	Spain	51	47/48	Pakistan	14
21	India	48	47/48	Indonesia	14
22/23	Japan	46	49	Colombia	13
22/23	Argentina	46	50	Venezuela	12
24	Iran	41	51	Panama	11
25	Jamaica	39	52	Equador	8
26/27	Brazil	38	53	Guatemala	6

Table 2.6   Business areas affected by individualism.

Low individualism	High individualism
Involvement of individuals with organizations primarily moral	Involvement of individuals with organizations primarily calculative
Employees expect organizations to look after them like family – and can become very alienated if organization dissatisfies them	Organizations are not expected to look after employees from the cradle to the grave
Organization has great influence on members' well-being	Organization has moderate influence on members' well-being
Employees expect organization to defend their interests	Employees are expected to defend their own interests
Promotion from inside and based on seniority	Promotion from inside and outside, and based on market value
Less concern with fashion in management ideas	Managers try to be up-to-date and endorse modern management ideas
Policies and practices vary according to relations	Policies and practices apply to all
Belief in group decisions	Belief in individual decisions
Emphasis on belonging to organization; membership ideal	Emphasis on individual initiative and achievement; leadership ideal
Private life is invaded by organizations and clans to which you belong; opinions are predetermined	Everyone has a right to a private life and their opinion

Source: Adapted from Hofstede G. (1984). *Culture's Consequences: International Differences in Work-Related Values*, abridged edn. Thousand Oaks, CA: Sage Publications Inc. Reproduced with permission of McGraw-Hill.

> # Box 2.3   Difference in work ethos between an individualist and a collectivist society
>
> Christopher Earley, an American management researcher, gave 48 management trainees from southern China and a matched group of 48 management trainees from the USA an 'in-basket task' consisting of 40 separate items requiring between two and five minutes each (Earley, 1989). The tasks involved such activities as writing memos, evaluating plans and rating job candidates' application forms. Half of the participants from each country were given an individual goal of 20 items; the other half were given a group goal of 200 items to be completed in one hour by 10 people. In addition, half of the participants from either country, both from the group and from the individual goal subsets, were asked to mark each item with their name; the other half turned them in anonymously.
>
> The Chinese, collectivist, participants performed best when operating with a group goal *and* anonymously. They performed worst when operating individually and with their name marked on their work. The individualist American participants performed best when operating individually and with their work attributed to them personally, and performed very poorly when operating as a group and anonymously.

Masculinity/femininity

These values concern the extent of emphasis on work goals (earnings, advancement) and assertiveness, as opposed to personal goals (friendly atmosphere, getting along with the boss and others) and nurturance. The first set of values is thought to be associated with males and the second more with females. According to Hofstede's definitions, masculine societies define gender roles more rigidly than feminine societies. For example, more masculine societies would happily have occupations restricted to men or to women only, whereas in feminine societies women may drive trucks or be surgeons while men may more easily be nurses or house husbands. Of the countries covered by Hofstede's research, Scandinavian countries are the most feminine, the USA slightly masculine, and Japan and Austria the most highly masculine. In both of these latter countries, women are generally expected to stay at home and care for the children without working outside the home, especially in their middle years. In Sweden women are expected to work and both parents are offered leave to care for newborn children. Women both on Volvo's assembly line and as top executives have been accepted as unexceptional for decades.

Table 2.7   Masculinity (MAS) scores.

Score rank	Country or region	MAS score	Score rank	Country or region	MAS score
1	Japan	95	27	Brazil	49
2	Austria	79	28	Singapore	48
3	Venezuela	73	29	Israel	47
4/5	Italy	70	30/31	Indonesia	46
4/5	Switzerland	70	30/31	West Africa	46
6	Mexico	69	32/33	Turkey	45
7/8	Ireland (Republic of)	68	32/33	Taiwan	45
			34	Panama	44
7/8	Jamaica	68	35/36	Iran	43
9/10	UK	66	35/36	France	43
9/10	West Germany	66	37/38	Spain	42
11/12	Philippines	64	37/38	Peru	42
11/12	Colombia	64	39	East Africa	41
13/14	South Africa	63	40	Salvador	40
13/14	Equador	63	41	South Korea	39
15	USA	62	42	Uruguay	38
16	Australia	61	43	Guatemala	37
17	New Zealand	58	44	Thailand	34
18/19	Greece	57	45	Portugal	31
18/19	Hong Kong	57	46	Chile	28
20/21	Argentina	56	47	Finland	26
20/21	India	56	48/49	Yugoslavia	21
22	Belgium	54	48/49	Costa Rica	21
23	Arab countries	53	50	Denmark	16
24	Canada	52	51	Netherlands	14
25/26	Malaysia	50	52	Norway	8
25/26	Pakistan	50	53	Sweden	5

Table 2.8   Business areas affected by masculinity.

Low masculinity	High masculinity
Less occupational segregation by gender	Some occupations are typically male, others female
Greater belief in equality of the sexes	Belief in inequality of the sexes
Some young men and women want careers, others do not	Young men expect to make a career; those who do not see themselves as failures
Organizations should not interfere with people's private lives	Organizational interests are a legitimate reason for interfering with people's private lives
More women in more qualified and better-paid jobs	Fewer women in more qualified and better-paid jobs
Lower job stress	Higher job stress
Less industrial conflict	More industrial conflict
Appeal of job restructuring permitting group integration	Appeal of job restructuring permitting individual achievement

Source: Adapted from Hofstede G. (1984). *Culture's Consequences: International Differences in Work-Related Values*, abridged edn. Thousand Oaks, CA: Sage Publications Inc. Reproduced with permission of McGraw-Hill.

Hofstede's work was based upon the analysis of over 100,000 responses to a questionnaire issued by IBM in its heydays during the 1970s. Hofstede did not invent these dimensions, but through deep analysis of the relationships between the answers to this questionnaire, he found they explained many of the differences that were evident between the widespread offices of what was essentially a very unifying global culture. IBM at the time was the most successful company in the world. These dimensions and Hofstede's tables of country positions in them are now recognized by all those who have any professional exposure to multicultural affairs. But there are still those who can profit from examining their implications in greater depth. One factor Hofstede continues to emphasize is that you cannot value values. From any one national's position, other nationals can seem strange. If they are seen because of this difference to be worse, then this strange difference will never become better understood.

Later work by the group of researchers in Hong Kong calling itself the Chinese Culture Connection found that by asking questions about work culture which Chinese might choose to ask instead of those used by IBM, three of Hofstede's dimensions were again revealed, but that uncertainty avoidance disappeared, and was replaced by an altogether different dimension, originally called Confucian dynamism. This dimension featured such factors as long-term versus short-term, thrift versus conspicuous expenditure and truth as an absolute versus truth as dependent upon who speaks. This latter case anticipates universalism versus particularism which we will explore next.

Hofstede's work provides an important framework in which to consider the effects of cultural differences on managing cultural differences; especially in terms of understanding people's conceptions of an organization, the mechanisms that are considered appropriate in controlling and coordinating the activities within it, and the roles and relations of its members. Another compelling description of how cultures differ has been developed by a Dutch economist and consultant, Fons Trompenaars. Encouraged by Hofstede, and building primarily from the work of Kluckhohn and Strodtbeck on value orientations (Kluckhorn and Stodtbeck, 1961), Charles Hampden-Turner's dilemma theory (Hampden-Turner, 1983), and Talcott Parsons's work in the 1950s, Trompenaars's research revealed seven dimensions of culture. Five of Trompenaars's dimensions will be discussed in this book because of their relevance to issues considered here. They provide another useful way for managers to consider how cultural differences affect organizations and management practices.

Fons Trompenaars's research

Over a 10-year period, Trompenaars administered research question-naires to over 15,000 managers from 28 countries. The relative positions of each country for each of the dimensions that he defined are based on the responses of at least 500 managers. Responses of 23 countries are included in this report. The country abbreviations are given below.

Box 2.4 Trompenaars's country abbreviations

Abbreviation	Country	Abbreviation	Country
ARG	Argentina	IDO	Indonesia
AUS	Austria	ITA	Italy
BEL	Belgium	JPN	Japan
BRZ	Brazil	MEX	Mexico
CHI	China	NL	Netherlands
CIS	Former Soviet	SIN	Singapore
	Union	SPA	Spain
CZH	Czechoslovakia	SWE	Sweden
FRA	France	SWI	Switzerland
GER	Germany	THA	Thailand
	(excluding	UK	United Kingdom
	former GDR)	USA	United States
HK	Hong Kong	VEN	Venezuela

The five dimensions that are most relevant to the business areas discussed in this book are as follows.

(1) Universalism versus particularism: societal versus personal obligation.
(2) Individualism versus collectivism: personal versus group goals.
(3) Neutral versus affective relationships: emotional orientation in relationships.
(4) Specific versus diffuse relationships: degree of involvement in relationships.
(5) Achievement versus ascription: legitimation of power and status.

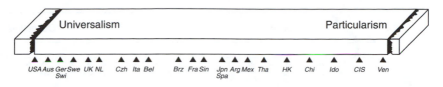

Figure 2.5   Universalism versus particularism. (*Source*: Adapted from Trompenaars, 1993)

Universalism versus particularism

Universalism applies where people believe that what is true and good can be discovered, defined and 'applied' everywhere. Particularism is said to prevail where the unique circumstances and relationships are more important considerations in determining what is right and good than abstract rules.

A clear example of this dimension in business is the role of the contract in different cultures. While weighty contracts tend to be a way of life in universalist cultures, more particularist cultures tend to rely on relationships with people they hold in high regard for enforcement of a deal. Encounters between universalist and particularist business people may result in both sides being sceptical of each other's trustworthiness. The universalist business person might think, 'How can you trust them [a particularist], they will always help their friends!' A particularist might think of a universalist, 'You cannot trust them, they would not even help a friend!'

The distribution of scores across the countries from which this scale was drawn shows a separation between East and West, and between North and South, notoriously the two divides that show up most in any global political or organizational issue (see Figure 2.5).

Table 2.9   Business areas affected by universalism/particularism.

Universalism	Particularism
Focus is more on rules than on relationships	Focus is more on relationships than on rules
Legal contracts are readily drawn up	Legal contracts are readily modified
A trustworthy person is the one who honours their 'word' or contract	A trustworthy person is the one who honours changing circumstances
There is only one truth or reality, that which has been agreed to	There are several perspectives on reality relative to each participant
A deal is a deal	Relationships evolve

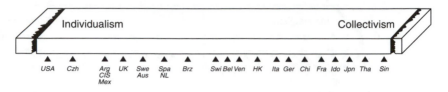

Figure **2.6** Individualism versus collectivism. (*Source*: Adapted from Trompenaars, 1993)

Individualism versus collectivism

This is familiar from Hofstede's work described previously. Essentially it concerns how groups have resolved the problem: does a person regard himself or herself primarily as an individual or primarily as part of a group? Furthermore, should society focus on individuals so that they can contribute to society as and if they wish, or is it more important to consider the collectivity first since it is shared by many individuals?

Within more collectivist societies, the particular group with which individuals choose to identify varies a great deal. It could be their trade union, their family, their nation, their corporation, their religion, their profession or the state apparatus. For example, the French tend to identify with *La France*, *La Famille*, *Le Cadre*; the Japanese with Japan and with the corporation; members of the former Eastern bloc with the Communist Party; and the Irish with the Roman Catholic Church.

International management is seriously affected by individualist or collectivist preferences within various countries. Negotiations, decision-making and motivation are the most critical areas. Practices such as promotion for recognized achievements and pay-for-performance, for example, assume that individuals seek to be distinguished within the group and that their colleagues approve of this happening. They also rest on the assumption that the contribution of any one member to a common task is easily distinguishable and that no problems arise from singling them out for praise. None of this may be true in more collectivist cultures.

Table 2.10 Business areas affected by individualism/collectivism.

Individualism	*Collectivism*
More frequent use of 'I' and 'me'	More frequent use of 'we'
In negotiations, decisions typically made on the spot by a representative	Decisions typically referred back by delegate to the organization
People ideally achieve alone and assume personal responsibility	People ideally achieve in groups which assume joint responsibility
Holidays taken in pairs, or even alone	Holidays taken in organized groups or with extended family

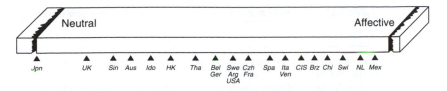

Figure 2.7   Neutral versus affective relationships. (*Source*: Adapted from Trompenaars, 1993)

Neutral versus affective relationships

All human beings have emotions, but this dimension concerns the different contexts and ways that cultures choose to *express* emotions. In affective cultures, expressing emotions openly is more 'natural', whereas in more neutral cultures people believe that emotions should be held in check so as not to cloud issues or give the appearance of being out of control.

There is a tendency for neutral cultures to consider anger, delight or intensity in the workplace as 'unprofessional'. Conversely, affective cultures would probably regard their neutral colleagues as emotionally dead, or as hiding their true feelings behind a mask of deceit. This dimension determines two fundamental questions:

(1)   Should emotion be *exhibited* in business relations?
(2)   Is emotion a corrupting influence on objectivity and reason?

Americans tend to exhibit emotion yet separate it from 'objective' and 'rational' decisions. Italians and southern European nations in general tend to exhibit and *not* to separate. Dutch and Swedes tend *not* to exhibit and to separate. Once again, there is nothing 'good' or 'bad' about these differences. You could argue that emotions held in check will twist judgements despite all efforts to be 'rational'. Or you could argue that emotions make it harder for anyone present to think straight. But as discussed in Chapter 1, the whole notion of rationality as a category of thought separate from other kinds of thought and emotion is a particular cultural preference. It is clear that even apparently scientific 'objectivity' cannot be separated from the particular cultural context in which it is embedded.

In Hofstede's model, the willingness to express emotion is seen as part of uncertainty avoidance. In his view, one reason for the need to manage uncertainty is a greater indigenous anxiety, a more prevalent fear of the unknown; this implies greater emotional volatility and therefore expressiveness. Since it is only one component, however, relative comparisons of scores are not easy to make.

Table 2.11 Business areas affected by neutral/affective relationships.

Affective	Neutral
Show immediate reactions either verbally or non-verbally	Opaque emotional state
Expressive face and body signals	Do not readily express what they think or feel
At ease with physical contact	Embarrassed or awkward at public displays of emotion
	Discomfort with physical contact outside 'private' circle
Raise voice readily	Subtle in verbal and non-verbal expressions

Specific versus diffuse relationships

This dimension deals with the degree of involvement individuals are comfortable with in dealing with other people. Every individual has various levels to their personality, from a more public level to the inner, more private level. However, there can be cultural differences in the relative size of people's public and private 'spaces' and also in the degree to which they feel comfortable sharing those parts of their personality with other people. In more specific cultures, Trompenaars says people tend to have a larger public area and a smaller private area. They prefer to keep their private life separate, guarding it very closely. In more diffuse cultures, the private 'space' is usually larger while the public area is smaller and somewhat more carefully guarded. While diffuse cultures may come across as cool initially, once in the more closely guarded public space, the private space is more accessible than in specific cultures. In other words, the whole individual tends to be involved in relationships in diffuse cultures.

For example, the circle diagrams in Figure 2.9 compare the more specific North Americans with the more diffuse Germans. North Americans are characterized by a small, intimate private layer that is well separated from the more public outer layers. In Germany, on the other hand, personality structures are characterized by a large private area

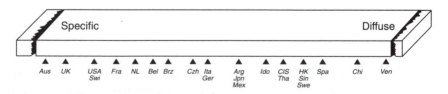

Figure 2.8 Specific versus diffuse relationships. (*Source*: Adapted from Trompenaars, 1993)

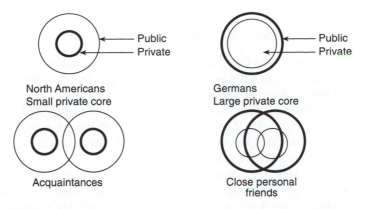

Figure 2.9 Privacy. (*Source*: Adapted from Trompenaars, 1993)

separated from a relatively small public layer. This means, for example, that it is not uncommon for German business colleagues to interact for years on a formal name basis while in the USA the norm is to be on a first-name basis immediately. To Americans, Germans seem reserved and difficult to get to know, while Germans may consider Americans intrusive and disrespectful.

Doing business with a culture more diffuse than your own appears very time consuming. In specific cultures, business can be done in a mental subdivision called 'commerce' or 'work', which is kept apart from the rest of life. In diffuse cultures, everything is connected to everything else. Your business partner may wish to know where you went to school, who your friends are, what you think of life, politics, art, literature and music. This is not 'a waste of time' because such preferences reveal character and form friendships. They also make deception near to impossible. The initial investment in building relationships is as important, if not more so, than the *deal* in some cultures.

Table 2.12 Business areas affected by specific/diffuse relationships.

Specific	*Diffuse*
More 'open' public space, more 'closed' private space	More 'closed' public space, but, once in, more 'open' private space
Appears direct, open and extrovert	Appears indirect, closed and introvert
'To the point' and often appears abrasive	Often evades issues and 'beats about the bush'
Highly mobile	Low mobility
Separates work and private life	Work and private life are closely linked
Varies approach to fit circumstances, especially with use of titles (for example, Herr Doktor Müller at work is Hans in social environments or in certain business meetings)	Consistent in approach, especially with use of titles (for example, Herr Doktor Müller is Herr Doktor Müller in any setting)

Achievement versus ascription

The last of the five Trompenaars cultural dimensions relevant to organizations deals with how status and power in a society are determined. Each society is presented both with characteristics assumed by a person as a birthright and with those that are left to be filled in through competition, personal effort or luck. Status can be based either on what someone does, or on what someone is. Cultures differ in the ways they have solved this dilemma.

In achievement-oriented countries, business people are evaluated by how well they perform an allocated function. Relationships are functionally specific. I relate to a colleague as, say, a sales manager. The justification of my role lies in the sales records. Another person in that role must be expected to be compared with me and I with that person. Success is universally defined as increased sales. My relationship to manufacturing, R&D, planning and so on is *instrumental*. I either sell what they have developed, manufactured and planned, or I do not. I *am* my functional role.

In ascriptive cultures, status is attributed to those who 'naturally' evoke admiration from others, that is older people, males, highly qualified people and/or people skilled in a particular technology or project deemed to be of national importance. To show respect for status is to assist the people so distinguished to fulfil the expectations society has of them. The status is generally independent of a task or specific function. The individual is particular and not easily compared with others. His (or her) performance is partly determined by the loyalty and affection shown him by subordinates and which he, in turn, displays. He (and in ascriptive cultures it is generally males who are in the positions of power) *is* the organization in the sense of personifying it and wielding its power.

While achievement-oriented organizations justify their hierarchies by claiming that senior people 'achieve more' for the organization because their authority, justified by skill and knowledge, benefits the organization, ascription-oriented organizations justify their hierarchies

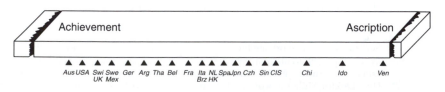

Figure   2.10   Achievement   versus   ascription.   (*Source*:   Adapted   from Trompenaars, 1993)

as central to creating the power to get things done. This may consist of power *over* people and be coercive, or it may consist of power *through* people and be participative. There is great variation within ascriptive cultures in the form that power takes. Whatever form power takes, the ascription of status to people is intended to be exercized as power and that power is supposed to enhance the effectiveness of the organization.

Achievement versus ascription has no direct match in Hofstede's terms. High power distance environments would be more likely to contain the ascriptive assumption. Those oriented towards the masculine would be places where the achievement orientation should flourish. But again there is no direct linkage between the two.

Culture and Dutchmen

It should not escape your notice that the two most prominent presenters of models of national culture in the past generation have both been Dutch and have both used bipolar dimensions as a means of communicating their models, each based upon a questionnaire response.

Trompenaars started with dimensions, mostly taken from Talcott Parsons, and produced questions based upon short value-laden dilemmas to produce the spread of national responses. Hofstede took existing data, and arrived at his four original dimensions through regression, then named the dimensions which arose using existing expressions.

For the novice intercultural enquirer, the two could have offered a more conveniently integratable model, but each gives something different to the experienced. The major dimensions which distinguish nations wishing to work closer together without abandoning or de-emphasizing their differences would seem to be:

- Power distance: how convinced are people that differences in power are given and accepted?
- Uncertainty avoidance: how much are people prepared to deal with the unexpected?
- Collectivism/individualism: which carries most weight – the individual or the group?
- Universalism/particularism: which has the greatest impact – the rule of law or the rule of the person who makes it?

These four dimensions should help managers most to identify how to create global competitiveness from diversity.

Summary

Culture is difficult to measure and to discuss because it involves shared ways of perceiving the world that members of a group take for granted. Culture is learned, and can be considered only relative to other cultures. There is no absolute right or wrong in cultural preferences.

Although there are different levels of cultural programming, national culture gives people their basic assumptions and values, that is, their ways of viewing the world. Other levels of programming are more about practices or ways of doing things. Because these are learned at such an early age and remain unquestioned, however, often throughout life, national cultural values are more difficult to change than other levels of culture.

In order to grasp better the impact of culture on international business, a few researchers have come up with ways of describing categories of differences in national cultures. Two Dutchmen, Hofstede and Trompenaars, have promoted the most expressive and popular of these. Their dimensions, which are presented in this chapter, do help to clarify some of the most important ways in which cultures differ and how those differences affect organizations generally. They provide a useful framework for managers to understand some of the differences they encounter in doing business and managing across cultures.

What becomes clear in the following chapters is that managers can more successfully manage differences in culture if they:

(1) Understand their own cultural biases and assumptions.
(2) Consider the reasons why different cultures' ways of doing things make sense in the light of their cultural assumptions.
(3) View cultural assumptions and ways of doing things not as irrecon-cilable differences, but rather as different starting points that can be integrated to develop uniquely competitive solutions.

References

Adler N.J. (1986). *International Dimensions of Organizational Behavior*. Belmont, California: PWS-Kent Publishing Company

Earley C.P. (1989). Social Loafing and Collectivism: A Comparison of the United States and the People's Republic of China, *Administrative Science Quarterly*, **34**, 565–581

Hall E.T. (1973). *The Silent Language*. New York: Doubleday

Hampden-Turner C. (1983). Is there a new paradigm? A tale of two concepts. *Personnel Management Review*, **56**

Hofstede G. (1984). *Culture's Consequences: International Differences in Work-Related Values*. Beverly Hills, California: Sage Publications

Hofstede G. (1991). *Cultures and Organizations: Software of the Mind*. London: McGraw-Hill

The Independent (1991). 31 December, p. 3

International Herald Tribune (1990). 11 December, p. 11

Kluckhohn F. and Strodtbeck F.L. (1961). *Variations in Value-Orientations*. Connecticut: Greenwood Press

Laurent A. (1989). A cultural view of organizational change. In *Human Resource Management in International Firms: Change, Globalization, Innovation* (Evans P., Doz Y. and Laurent A., eds.) London: Macmillan, pp. 83-94

Trompenaars F. (1993). *Riding the Waves of Culture*. London: The Economist Books

3

The strategic value of cultural differences

Competitive requirements of internationalization

Emerging along with increasingly global markets and global competition are new organizational forms and competitive requirements which absolutely demand that managers pay attention to differences in national culture. The internationalization of business is not something that is yet to happen, nor is it a route which businesses can *choose* to follow. The distinctions between domestic and international markets are crumbling fast in virtually every part of the world. Almost any kind of uni-national business is seeing, or will very soon see, its markets invaded by foreign players. These companies may still think of themselves as purely domestic operations, yet they are nonetheless directly experiencing the impact of internationalization.

A broader mind-set

The old definitions of international business are now defunct; terms such as 'exporting' and 'importing', 'domestic' and 'overseas' are now largely irrelevant. They encourage a mind-set that is in danger of being insular and limited by obsolete boundaries and distinctions. Instead, many companies are searching for a new language; a fresh way of perceiving their environments; more complex and fluid organizational structures; new strategies and new leadership styles. Rosabeth Moss Kanter identifies the search for a new business mind-set as one of the most important changes happening today. She points to the 'triumph of process over structure' as a key indication of this change. 'What is important is not how responsibilities are divided but how people can pull together to pursue new opportunities' (Barnham and Devine, 1993). Whatever the current organizational structure or industry, there is a need to break down compartmentalized thinking – whether between different business disciplines, products, markets or cultures – in order to adopt innovative business approaches.

More complex organizational forms

A 1989 survey of over 1500 top executives in 20 countries published by Korn/Ferry International and Columbia University Graduate School of Business attempted to establish the organizational priorities needed to equip multinational companies (MNCs) for the increasing demands of international business. One of the top six challenges these executives recognized was the inadequacy of home-based corporate structures to meet the demands of globalization and the increasing velocity of change (Redding and Baldwin, 1991). New organizational forms are required by the restructuring of world industry and commerce, and those forms demand that managers pay attention to cultural differences. For example, the 'transnational' organization, the form many internationally operating companies are moving towards, offers important strategic capabilities, but also creates a host of new managerial requirements. In their book *Managing Across Borders*, Christopher Bartlett of Harvard Business School and Sumantra Ghoshal of INSEAD assert that businesses need to organize themselves in a dramatically different way if they are to survive and flourish in the international business arena. Traditionally, the authors argue, the majority of companies have built their international operations around one of three strategies (Bartlett and Ghoshal, 1989):

(1)   Businesses such as Philips and General Electric have pursued a multinational strategy enabling them to establish a strong local presence through responding to different national market requirements.

(2)   The Japanese firms Kao and Matsushita have operated as global companies, making themselves fiercely competitive by achieving substantial cost advantages from centralized global-scale operations.

(3)   Ericsson and ITT have developed as international companies whose key strategic capability lies in exploiting parent-company knowledge through worldwide diffusion and adaptation.

Bartlett and Ghoshal's central argument is that significant businesses can no longer afford to base their strategy on a single focus. If companies are to cope with the complex international environment, they must have an equally complex and multi-faceted business strategy. Firms operating worldwide must pursue global, multinational and international strategies simultaneously. They must become what the authors call a transnational corporation. This organization has the following characteristics:

- *An integrated, networking structure.* Every part of the organization collaborates, shares information, solves problems and collectively implements strategy by forming an integrated network which shares decision-making and where components, products, resources, information and people flow freely between its interdependent units.
- *Dynamic decision-making.* There is a dynamic and integrative way of taking decisions through winning the agreement and commitment of every individual employee to the overall corporate agenda.
- *Adaptive coordination mechanisms.* A mix of control mechanisms are employed including highly formalized and institutionalized control mechanisms, centralized decision-making and socialization of a common corporate culture and shared perspective among managers.
- *Unique innovation capabilities.* Worldwide product responsibilities are allocated to different national subsidiaries according to their relative skills and strengths; and organizational learning is facilitated by fostering a flow of intelligence, ideas and knowledge around the organization.

Each of these characteristics implies a sophisticated understanding of and ability to manage successfully cultural differences.

Creating sustainable sources of competitive advantage

Other strategic developments similarly depend on the ability to manage cultural differences, especially the need to develop more sustainable competitive advantages from 'softer' effectiveness sources rather than 'harder' efficiency sources. The way in which firms compete is changing. In its simplified form, the argument runs as follows (Redding and Baldwin, 1991):

- In the early stages the winners are those who can get access to key resources (until anybody can).

- In the next stage, the winners are those who can master production efficiency (until anybody can).
- At this point the winners are those who can master market sensitivity and adaptiveness (until anybody can).
- In the final stages, the winners are those who can offer a distinct and unique product or service that the customer values (and – if this is based on, or delivered by virtue of, a distinct and unique corporate culture – then nobody else can).

In this way a company's culture, meaning its unique capabilities to manage and create value from its people, attitudes, shared values and cooperative behaviour, becomes an increasingly important strategic weapon.

Regardless of current organizational form, industry, size or culture, there is an opportunity to derive tangible benefits from cultural differences. Recognizing this possibility and acknowledging the points about what culture is and is not from Chapter 2, means that apart from preventing failures and mistakes from cultural misunderstandings and mismanagement, managers can begin to realize the potential advantages of using culture strategically. A few of the possibilities which will be explored in the following chapters include:

- Placing control for particular products, services or processes in national areas where the local culture has lead to unique strengths and capabilities.
- Using cultural differences in people's ways of solving problems to speed up and improve product cycle times.
- Creating multi-cultural teams to approach difficult problems where there is a need to break down assumptions about how something has to be done.
- Anticipating the potential areas of conflict and of advantage in cross-border alliances.
- Developing more effective global and local advertising and marketing strategies.

Approaches to managing cultural differences

In the course of the research for this book, it became clear that there are various approaches international companies have been using to manage cultural differences. It also became apparent that the approach employed tends to reflect the national cultural values and assumptions of the company's country of origin. By understanding how cultural assumptions determine the management solutions recognized as 'correct' or even possible, we can broaden our perspective about the range of approaches available and will be in a better position to adopt the most appropriate strategies for particular problems and environments.

Organizations throughout the world must have three basic characteristics if they are to survive and prosper. They need:

(1) Cohesion among their members about common purposes.
(2) Cooperation between various parts of the organization.
(3) Some form of hierarchical order that is recognized as legitimate, acceptable, proper and preferably motivating.

These universal principles do not change, but the way in which they are interpreted is highly variable.

Certain ways of handling the issues set out above are preferred in certain societies and therefore become the local norm. As these patterns become discernible, it can be surmised that the environment decides the favoured business recipe. However, the categories of society are not black and white and the key word remains 'tendencies', although these are often extremely strong. For example, the *chaebol* is distinctly and uniquely Korean, while the divisionalized multinational bureaucracy is identifiably Western. Each society contains variety, of course, but it also fosters the crystallization of one dominant and representative type of organization (Redding and Baldwin, 1991).

Two of the cultural dimensions discussed in Chapter 2, power distance and uncertainty avoidance, are useful in understanding how culture influences the solutions chosen about how to organize. Culture can determine the kinds of structures and coordination mechanisms that are thought to be 'natural' and 'right'. Implicit cultural values will also influence the assumptions about the extent to which differences in culture have an impact on organizations and the extent to which they are perceived as being 'manageable', 'unmanageable' or best ignored.

Nancy Adler and M. Maruyama have both explored the issue of organizational structure and cultural assumptions. Adler developed the model shown in Figure 3.1 from original research conducted with Fariborz Ghadar (Adler, 1986). Maruyama identified a model of how organizations manage cultural differences based on both alternative assumptions about the impact of cultural diversity on the organization and the stages of moving from international, multidomestic and multinational to the global firm.

Critical examination of this model of cultural assumptions and organizational structure stage by stage can be of real help to firms growing rapidly towards a global status.

Structure: multidomestic
Cultural assumption: diversity has no impact

Building a strong corporate culture internationally

Building a strong corporate culture is a topic that has generated a great deal of comment. Following the explosive sales of Peters and Waterman's *In Search of Excellence*, many believed in and wrote about culture in a way that implicitly assumed that a strong corporate culture would lead to superior performance. Recent attempts to explore the link between a strong corporate culture and financial success, however, have left this assumption in question. Moreover, the dangers of pursuing a strong singular culture across all national boundaries as a major strategy are considerable: a tendency for 'group think', a propensity to focus inward, an unquestioning acceptance of the status quo and, in extreme cases, blind arrogance. Another problem with attempting to extend a common corporate culture throughout a globally operating organization is that in distilling the message down to the basic tenets which can presumably be understood everywhere, the least common denominator message becomes basically indistinguishable from any other corporate culture. In other words, the uniqueness of the message is taken out in order to promote a simple, easily understandable cultural statement.

The assumptions behind adopting this strategy are those given above for an international firm. Homogeneity is viewed as basic and natural and management believes there is one best way to manage. A case that illustrates the approach of a company attempting to build a very strong international corporate culture is the Swedish furniture company, Ikea (see Case 3.1).

Case 3.1 Ikea

Ikea is a privately held furniture retailing giant with a turnover in excess of Skr22 billion ($3.7 billion). Now the world's largest international home furnishing chain, its reach has spread to 96 outlets in 24 countries. Adding to that complexity is the number of articles it sells – over 11,500 with 1750 suppliers in 53 countries. How it manages this network of diversity is unique and much talked about. It seems to be an ideological glue of sorts; a very strong corporate culture based on the roots of the organization's founder.

continues

continued

The leaders of Ikea believe it is critical for an organization to have a very strong set of values for people to believe in. Ikea's head of North American Operations, Goran Carstedt, explained why.

'In the new reality of globally operating companies, you have to get the energy from the outside in, and not in the traditional way, so to say, steering from the top, where you dictate from headquarters. The old notion of running a business from top down, that is gone.

'The most important distinction between the organizations that will make it and those that will not, is to understand this. Instead, you have to have other ways of keeping the organization together. And that has to do with something else. The steering, so to say, must be more ideological; related to some basic values. You have to have something in common and feel like you are valued, that you want to participate. Then, I think you have a glue. Because if you are just out there to earn money, like the normal holding companies... I just do not see how that can turn people on.

'Personally, I want to be part of a company that stands for something.'

And what Ikea stands for is *very* Swedish. Even the company name is based on the initials of the founder's name and the farm and parish where he grew up:

Ingvar
Kamprad } founder's name

Elmtaryd   his farm

Agunnaryd   his parish

'The area of Sweden that Ingvar comes from', Mr Carstedt explained, 'was very rocky, hard farm land. It was not a good place to grow things, but the farmers did. They broke ground and made things grow. So the values of that region of Sweden, called Småland, are all about thrift, no waste, being careful with your resources and so on. That is very much the basis of Ikea's culture.' Of course, this is also fairly typical of Swedish culture in general. 'In Sweden,' he continued, 'we even have a law which reminds us of our own insignificance.' Another important element of the Ikea culture: 'humbleness'.

Everything about the company is organized around these core values, which are basically the same in every culture in which it operates. The company uses extensive screening and hiring procedures to select people, in each country, whose *personal* values fit with Ikea's *corporate* values. All other aspects of the company, too, are designed to reflect and reinforce these values (see below).

continues

continued

Management ideas, practices and concepts	Values reflected
Business idea 'We shall offer a wide range of home furnishing items of good design and function, at prices so low that the majority of people can afford to buy them.'	Egalitarianism
Management practices Anti-bureaucratic week – managers spend a week working in stores serving customers, working in the restaurant, and so on.	Simplicity 'Humbleness'
Only seven levels between president and entry level	Hard work
Casual dress at all levels of the organization	
Coach-class travel for everyone	
Travel on own time	
Cheap hotel rooms, even for the chairman	
Human resource idea Described in an internal hand-out: 'To give down-to-earth, straightforward people the possibility to grow, both as individuals and in their professional roles.'	No waste
Human resource practices Hiring young people not yet 'corrupted' by other company cultures	
Very selective hiring: finding people in any culture who have similar values	
Production/Design concepts Design products that are simple, straightforward, 'young at heart', easy to live with and durable	
Selling concepts Outlets all the same colour: blue and yellow like the Swedish flag	
Combine furniture, showroom and warehouse	
Minimal sales staff	
Customers load and put the merchandise together themselves	

Ikea recognizes that cultural differences can lead to barriers and misunderstandings, but that, on the other hand, they can be a tremendous source of advantage. 'You need to test your ideas in relation to the realities of other cultures,' Mr Carstedt explained. In the USA, he thought perhaps that meant that over time they would add a few stars and stripes to the way they do things, but the philosophy would be the same.

The thing about this way of working is that 'when you have something that is based on ideas and values, they have always to be discussed.

continues

continued

An idea is dead if it is not discussed. So you have to invite constant discussion and debate on your ideas and values.' Ikea does this in a variety of ways. Most visible are the 'Ikea Way' seminars for all employees where the company's roots and values are explained and discussed. There are also employee trips to Sweden where they visit the shed where the founder first started the business. Some employees even become 'ambassadors' of the culture.

Mr Carstedt believes that such 'ideological glue' can work, and indeed, to be competitive, must work in every successful globally operating business.

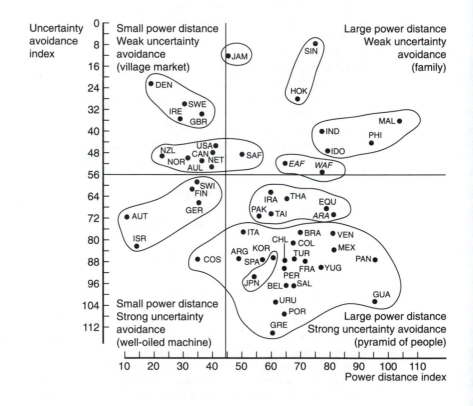

Figure 3.2 Uncertainty avoidance and power distance scores. (For key to country abbreviations, see Figure 2.4.)

As would be expected, Ikea's strategy for managing cultural differences very much reflects the national cultural values of its home country. As Goran Carstedt, head of North American Operations, described, the corporate values and practices are built around such Swedish values as egalitarianism, frugality, hard work, simplicity, caring about individuals and so on. Looking back to some of the cultural dimensions discussed in Chapter 2, Sweden and most of the other Scandinavian countries have both a small power distance and a weak uncertainty avoidance (see Figure 3.2).

The implicit model of the organization typical of people from this cultural profile is the village market, and the tendency is to use standardization of skills as a primary control mechanism. Sweden is also relatively individualistic, and the most 'feminine' scoring nation in Hofstede's study (see Figure 3.3). The implications are that they would tend to be very concerned with the individual and with creating a supportive, nurturing environment for individuals within the organization. The focus on 'belonging' and egalitarianism are directly related to this cultural

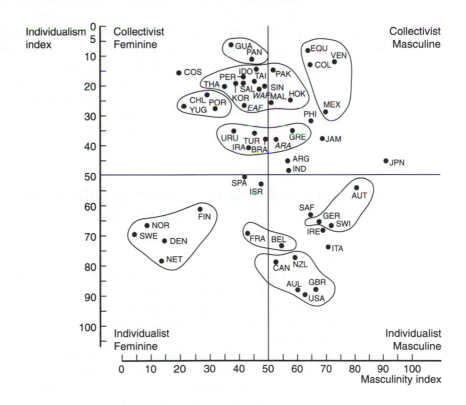

Figure 3.3 Individualism and masculinity/femininity scores. (For key to country abbreviations, see Figure 2.4.)

predisposition. It is interesting to note that Sweden is also relatively 'universalistic', and Ikea, being admittedly a very Swedish company, seems to have no real doubts that its solution is *the* correct formula for successful organizations in a global environment.

Although Mr Carstedt expressed the view that the old top-down notion of management is gone, Ikea's values and ways of working are rigidly defined, determine membership of the organization and are expected to be emulated in all its operations worldwide.

A recent attempt to explore the link between a strong corporate culture and financial success was made by John Kotter and James Heskett of Harvard Business School. In a study limited to American companies, they found that there is a positive relationship between a strong corporate culture and long-term economic performance, but that it is only a modest one (Kotter and Heskett, 1992). Upon closer examination of the higher-performing strong cultures, they found that these cultures emphasized concern for all the stakeholders related to the organization, and had other Ikea-like values such as simplicity, hard work, caring about individuals, and so on. Kotter and Heskett's findings reinforce the notion that it is the particular cultural values that determine the success of this strategy for managing cultural diversity, at least in markets with a similar cultural profile. However, there are drawbacks to applying this strategy globally. First, it diminishes the potential for building cultural synergies and second, it may fail in markets where it is not as easy to find people whose personal values match the values of the corporation. The more an organization insists on such homogeneity, the more likely it is to eliminate any of the constructive tension between cultures which can lead to important and innovative advantages.

Building a common technical or professional culture and relying on strong financial or planning systems

The next two strategies identified also correspond with the international organizational structure and assumptions of the model described at the beginning of this chapter. Building a common technical or professional culture, as the French firm Elf Aquitaine has done (see Case 3.2), or building a strong planning or systems means of control (see Case 3.3), both assume that technical or procedural mechanisms can overcome cultural differences.

The implicit assumption is clear: cultural diversity causes only problems but, rather than selecting a homogeneous workforce, differences can be minimized by drawing on technical or procedural 'objectivity'. These strategies are assumed to 'supersede' national cultural differences.

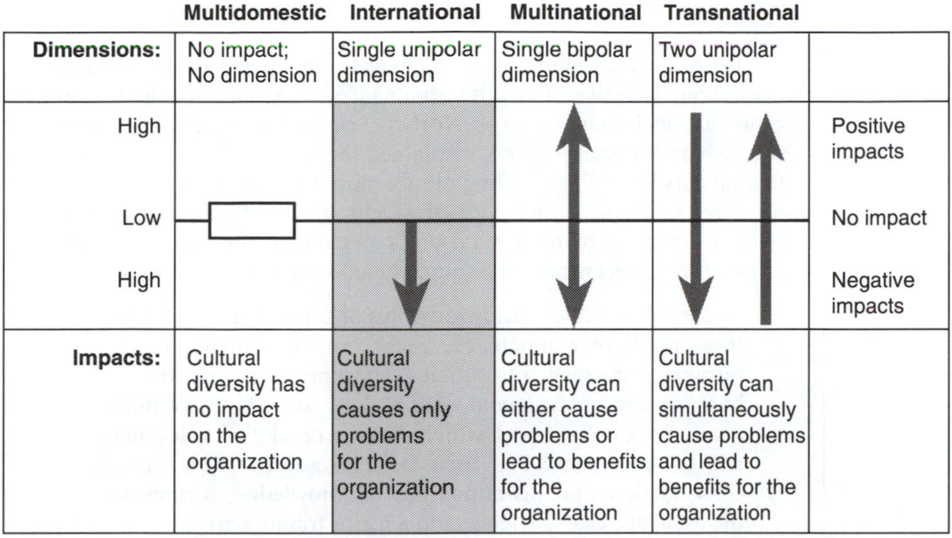

	Multidomestic	International	Multinational	Transnational	
Dimensions:	No impact; No dimension	Single unipolar dimension	Single bipolar dimension	Two unipolar dimension	
High					Positive impacts
Low					No impact
High					Negative impacts
Impacts:	Cultural diversity has no impact on the organization	Cultural diversity causes only problems for the organization	Cultural diversity can either cause problems or lead to benefits for the organization	Cultural diversity can simultaneously cause problems and lead to benefits for the organization	

Figure 3.4 International organizational structure and cultural assumptions. (*Source*: Adapted with permission from NTL Institute. Adler, 1983)

Case 3.2   Elf Aquitaine

Elf Aquitaine, over half of whose 89,000 employees work in Paris, operates in over 60 countries. Its business is segmented into Hydrocarbons (33%), Chemicals (40%) and Health, Beauty and Bio-activities (27%). With more than 700 subsidiaries around the world, its 1991 revenue was Fr175.5 billion.

Jacques Casanova, vice-president of human resources, explained how the group manages to create cohesion out of so much diversity: 'Technical knowledge, competence and skills are absolutely vital in our organization. They are the glue that holds our group together.' He described Elf Aquitaine not as a conglomerate 'but a large industrial group. Its success is due to the quality and competence of its people... We are federators, not centralizers. We never impose. We have only guidelines, which are to be seen as harmonizing principles. The group intends to maintain the highest professional standards in its specific areas of expertise. These are part of its core assets, and proficiency in them is crucial to staying competitive.'

continues

continued

Elf Aquitaine's emphasis on technical competence as the organizational bond is derived from the dominance of engineers in the organization and its French heritage. Norbert Fruythof, executive director of research and special projects, explained that this is why it is a culture that favours technological competence more than anything else.

Lasse Aga, executive vice-president of Elf Aquitaine Norway, related a concrete manifestation of its theme *unity through professionalism* within a decentralized organizational structure:

> 'We want to create worldwide pools of competence. To create these pools of competence, each company pursues human resource management policies appropriate to its line of business and environment. But it does so within a common Social Policy Statement which focuses on skill development and enhancement. The focus is on research programmes, consolidation and dissemination of knowledge, forums for the exchange of experience and a major training drive.'

The formal Social Policy Statement indicates that this skill enhancement is key to its other main priority of strengthening group cohesion. Professionalism in Elf Aquitaine seems to be expected to overcome cultural differences within the group. Mr Fruythof explained that 'cultural problems never occur when big objectives are at stake. As highly skilled and competent managers, we all have an understanding of our goals.'

Within the Exploration and Production divisions, Elf Aquitaine has realized encouraging results in the field of international team-building. According to Mr Casanova, international team-building has worked best within technological activities because it is exactly in that discipline that people feel united through a strong culture of technological competence. 'By paying so much attention to competence, development and enhancement, we have created a veritable community of skills that allows the group to offer those who possess them the chance to exercise their talents where they are most needed, while giving the group's subsidiaries their pick of help for solving unforeseen problems.'

The group's emphasis and reliance on competence and technical skills are also expressed through the initiative 'Know How 2000'. This is a joint plan between Elf's Production and Exploration divisions that qualitatively evaluates the skills that will be needed in their operations over the next ten years.

The strategy that Elf Aquitaine adopts reflects some of the more consistent and distinctive elements of French companies which they tend to retain as they internationalize: a focus on the intellectual, the rational and disciplined, structured planning.

Case 3.3   Emerson Electric

Emerson Electric is one of the USA's leading manufacturing corporations. With sales of $8.2 million, Emerson marked 36 years of improved earnings and earnings per share in 1993; its financial performance is matched by only a handful of manufacturing companies worldwide. From its corporate headquarters in St Louis, Missouri (in Mid-West USA), Emerson's operations span the globe, with manufacturing in 20 countries and sales offices in an additional 30. Having grown through acquisition, it is a highly decentralized organization with very little interaction between its 40 divisions.

How are cultural differences managed currently? Primarily by implementing a rigorous planning and reporting process. Charles F. Knight, chief executive officer, describes in a *Harvard Business Review* article what makes Emerson 'tick' (*Harvard Business Review*, 1992).

> 'Simply put, what makes us "tick" at Emerson is an effective management process. We believe we can shape our future through careful planning and strong follow-up. Our managers plan for improved results and execute to get them. Driving this process is a set of shared values, including involvement, intensity, discipline and persistence... Several assumptions underlie our management process. We believe, for example, that profitability is a state of mind. Experience tells us that if management concentrates on the fundamentals and constantly follows up, there is no reason why we can't achieve profits year after year.'

The shared values of the organization across cultures are financial. The 'ideological glue' at Emerson, rather than having to do with a set of beliefs about 'belonging' or a technical skills-based culture, is about meticulous planning, cost reduction and financial reporting. At a corporate level, there is little or no interaction between Emerson divisions within the same country. Corporate practice is to have local country managers in most overseas operations, and to leave these local managers responsible for the 'how' of meeting their targets. As many of Emerson's divisions are multinational organizations themselves, the management of cultural differences is, in a sense, pushed down to the operating level. At the corporate level, it means foreign operations dealing with only a handful of Americans from the corporate office in planning and tracking their results.

About their planning process, Mr Knight said:

> 'At Emerson, rigorous planning has been essential to the company's success since the 1950s. As CEO, more than half of

continues

continued

my time each year is blocked out strictly for planning. Other senior managers spend even more time in planning sessions... Each fiscal year, from November through June, selected corporate officers and I meet with the management of every division for a one- or two-day planning conference, usually held off-site. These division conferences are the culmination of our planning cycle. The mood is confrontational – by design... We want proof that a division is stretching to reach its goals, and we want to see the details of the actions division management believes will yield results. Our expectations are high, and the discussions are intense. A division president who comes to a planning conference poorly prepared has made a serious mistake.'

The requirements for each division and each operation are clear. Even the charts and graphs that must be used in the planning conferences are established by corporate headquarters. Time horizons and performance criteria are held constant for all operations across cultures. Mr Knight said:

'Nothing we do has a geographic or national basis. The sources of competitive success are the same in Japan, Germany, the USA, or any other strong manufacturing economy... We believe that planning will pay off if management implements it aggressively, that the results of the process will reward the intensity of the effort, and that people will respect and respond to tough challenges.'

Referring to the positions of France and the USA on Hofstede's dimensions of power distance and uncertainty avoidance, the Elf Aquitaine and Emerson cases are a perfect fit with these cultures' preferred organizational configuration and coordination mechanisms (see Figure 3.5). The implicit model of the organization in France tends to be the full bureaucracy, or pyramid of people. Coordination tends to be achieved through highly structured activities. By standardization of work processes and concentrating authority, the organization can specify who supplies what expertise from their position within the hierarchy. The preferred organizational form in the USA is the divisionalized company and standardizing outputs is the preferred mechanism of control. Emerson's focus on detailed planning and performance criteria is a typical example of this cultural combination at work.

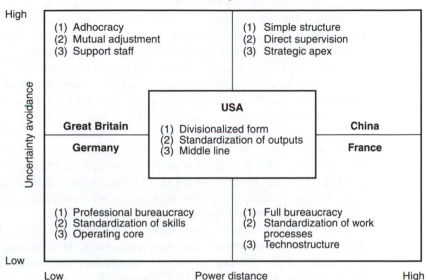

(1) Preferred configuration
(2) Preferred coordination mechanism
(3) Key part of organization

High

(1) Adhocracy
(2) Mutual adjustment
(3) Support staff

(1) Simple structure
(2) Direct supervision
(3) Strategic apex

Uncertainty avoidance

USA

Great Britain

(1) Divisionalized form
(2) Standardization of outputs
(3) Middle line

China

Germany

France

(1) Professional bureaucracy
(2) Standardization of skills
(3) Operating core

(1) Full bureaucracy
(2) Standardization of work processes
(3) Technostructure

Low

Low   Power distance   **High**

Organizations in general contain up to five distinct parts:
(1) The operating core (the people who do the work)
(2) The strategic apex (the top management)
(3) The middle line (the hierarchy in between)
(4) The technostructure (people in staff roles supplying ideas)
(5) The support staff (people in staff roles supplying services)

Organizations in general use one or more of five mechanisms for coordinating activities:
(1) Mutual adjustment (of people through informal communication)
(2) Direct supervision (by a hierarchical superior)
(3) Standardization of work processes (specifying the contents of work)
(4) Standardization of outputs (specifying the desired results)
(5) Standardization of skills (specifying the training required to perform the work)

Most organizations show one of five typical configurations:
(1) The simple structure. In this case, the key part is the strategic apex, and the coordinating mechanism is direct supervision.
(2) The machine bureaucracy. Key part: the technostructure. Coordinating mechanism: standardization of work processes.
(3) The professional bureaucracy. Key part: the operating core. Coordinating mechanism: standardization of skills.
(4) The divisionalized form. Key part: the middle line. Coordinating mechanism: standardization of outputs.
(5) The adhocracy. Key part: the support staff (sometimes with the operating core). Coordinating mechanism: mutual adjustment.

Figure 3.5   Preferred organizational configuration and coordination mechanisms.
(*Source*: Adapted from Hofstede, 1991)

An interesting contrast with the Ikea case is to compare Sweden, France and the USA on the dimension of 'masculinity/femininity', as defined by Hofstede (see Figure 3.3). While Sweden is the most feminine, France is roughly between it and the USA, which is relatively masculine. Masculine and feminine cultures create different management heroes and conceive of motivating people differently. The masculine manager is assertive, decisive and 'aggressive' – which carries a positive connotation in masculine countries. The hero is a lonely decision-maker who is after the hard facts, rather than a group discussion leader (Hofstede, 1991). Note Mr Knight's comment about planning meetings being 'confrontational by design'. In masculine cultures a 'humanized job' should give more opportunity for recognition, advancement and challenge. Mr Knight again: 'Our managers plan for improved results and execute to get them. Driving this process is a set of shared values, including involvement, intensity, discipline and persistence... We believe that people will respect and respond to tough challenges.'

The manager in a feminine culture is less visible, intuitive rather than decisive, and accustomed to seeking consensus. In feminine cultures a 'humanized job' should give more opportunity for mutual help and social contacts (Hofstede, 1991). Compare Mr Carstedt's remarks with Mr Knight's: '[To keep the organization together] you have to have something in common and feel like you are valued, that you want to participate. Then, I think you have a glue. Because if you are just out there to earn money, like the normal holding companies... I just do not see how that can turn people on. Personally, I want to be part of a company that stands for something.'

The assumption that they have found the 'right' way at all three organizations discussed so far seems to be dominant in cultures that are more universalist than particularist (see Chapter 2) – they assume that there is one best way that can be applied universally. They believe that what is 'rational' can be separated from relationships. Referring back to the dimension scores in Chapter 2, you would expect to find companies from Anglo-Saxon origins adopting such strategies. The assumption could then be that people's 'professional lives' could be governed by these 'objective' criteria, which may or may not be valid in the rest of their lives. Alternatively, it would seem that more particularist and diffuse cultures would be less likely to develop rigid or standardized systems to manage across cultures, and rather more likely to leave room for what they might see as more pervasive cultural considerations.

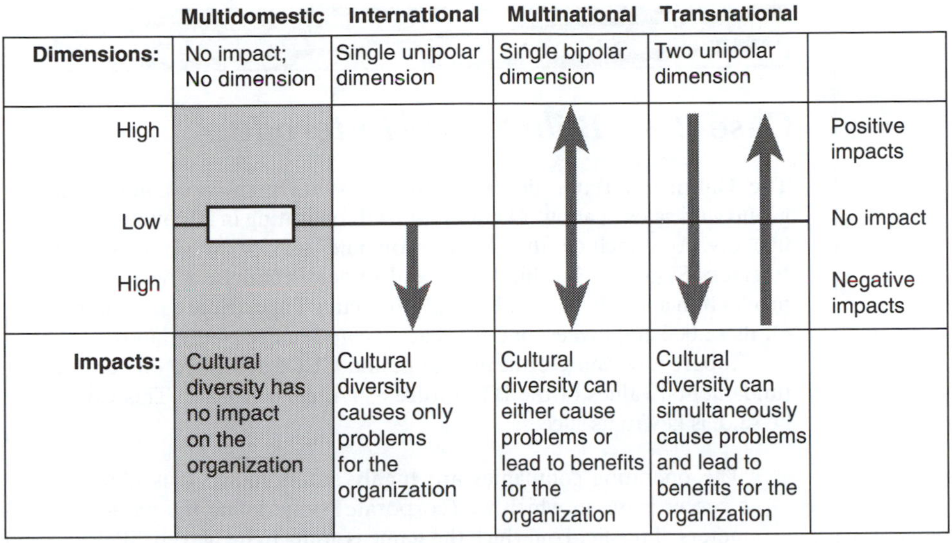

	Multidomestic	International	Multinational	Transnational	
Dimensions:	No impact; No dimension	Single unipolar dimension	Single bipolar dimension	Two unipolar dimension	
High					Positive impacts
Low					No impact
High					Negative impacts
Impacts:	Cultural diversity has no impact on the organization	Cultural diversity causes only problems for the organization	Cultural diversity can either cause problems or lead to benefits for the organization	Cultural diversity can simultaneously cause problems and lead to benefits for the organization	

Figure 3.6   Multidomestic organizational structure and cultural assumptions. (*Source*: Adapted with permission from NTL Institute. Adler, 1983)

Leaving each culture alone

Based on interviews with 'Western' companies, the last strategy identified for managing cultural differences is that of leaving each culture alone. The organizational analogy with this strategy is a multidomestic one, with the recognition of cultural diversity but without an attempt to control it or derive benefit from it (see Figure 3.6 and Case 3.4).

In part, BT's behaviour, described in Case 3.4, can be explained by the Netherlands' 'feminine' orientation towards a 'caring for', developmental spirit. Perhaps also the relative diversity of market makes the choice of multidomestic structure one which is conditioned by the purely pragmatic considerations of commercial success.

The case studies presented so far have represented international organizations originating from Western Europe and the USA. Asia/ Pacific offers a very different implicit model of the organization and different preferred control mechanisms.

Case 3.4   Bührmann-Tetterode

The Bührmann-Tetterode (BT) Group is a Dutch-based industrial group with sales of about $4 billion in 1991, operating in 20 countries. Its five divisions include the distribution and service of Graphic and Business Systems, Graphic Paper and Office Products, as well as the production and sale of Flexible and Protective Paper/Board packaging. Of its 13,000 employees, one-third are located in the Netherlands.

Robert F.W. van Oordt, president and CEO, described one of the fundamental values of the BT culture as *entrepreneurship*. This value, he said, is key to its success.

> 'The operating companies are highly autonomous. It is like a soccer game in which we (corporate) only define the parameters of the field on which the game is going to be played, like the colour of the grass. From there on, the companies do whatever they consider prudent, given the local market conditions. We have no strong prescriptions.'

According to Mr van Oordt, BT uses three vehicles to guide the performance of the operating companies:

(1)   Agreeing on an appropriate course of strategic direction, including clear quantitative and qualitative objectives.
(2)   Spelling out a set of limited authority limits for each level of management.
(3)   Maintaining an enhanced management information system, including open and regular exchanges of information at various levels, which provides information on the performance of each product and market combination within the product/market combinations and business units that make up the activities of the various operating companies.

The guidelines and systems that are developed centrally provide the framework for the operating companies. They are developed in close cooperation with BT's local managers and are implemented in such a way that they do not thwart the entrepreneurial spirit and the individual responsibility of the local companies.

BT's policy of hiring local managers for local operations reinforces the entrepreneurial spirit throughout the group. Mr van Oordt emphasized the group's orientation to respect the cultural aspects of the countries in which it operates. 'We try to minimize the influences from headquarters and aim at providing expert service on important issues only. Culturally, we want to be very local.'

Asia/Pacific models of organization

The position of all of the countries in the Asia/Pacific region on the cultural dimensions of individualism/collectivism and power distance is very different from the position of the most 'Western' industrialized countries. All Asia/Pacific societies are collectivist and all Western societies are individualist. In Asia a person's identity is heavily bound up with his or her relationships in a way that many Westerners find hard to understand – and even harder to experience. The Asian sense of being embedded in a network – and inextricable from it – contrasts sharply with the Western ideal of 'doing your own thing', 'being your own man', 'standing on your own two feet', and searching for personal self-fulfilment (Redding and Baldwin, 1991).

This is one of the deepest contrasts between East and West and is a result of long historical processes; the Western notion of democracy and individual freedom is simply one example of this difference. These deep-rooted attitudes affect organizations in a complex way, but the three basic features can be summarized as follows (Redding and Baldwin, 1991):

(1) The typical Pacific/Asian person has a strong sense of psychological dependency on a particular social grouping, which tends to dominate his or her motivation: for the Chinese, it is the family, and family business therefore predominates; among the Japanese, it is the work group. However, in both cases, individuals commonly place group interests above their personal interests.

(2) Inside an Asia/Pacific organization, a web of relationships grows based on unseen understandings about mutual obligation, which may interfere with what Westerners see as rational and objective decision-making.

(3) Relations between organizations are also networked and are commonly stronger than in the West. They produce complicated webs of alliances, many of which are informal and invisible, but capable of powerful effects in the interests of their members.

The other cultural dimension, power distance, also clearly divides East and West, although the distinction is less obvious than in the case of individualism. High power distance societies generally have a stable vertical order, the subtleties of which are often visible only to its members. It is often accompanied by a concern with titles, elaborate rituals of acknowledging precedence and long-term maintenance of ties of obligation. As all organizations are in essence vertical structures, the society's rules for authority become embedded in its business entities.

What do these cultural assumptions mean in terms of their preferred solutions for organizing and coordinating activities within organizations?

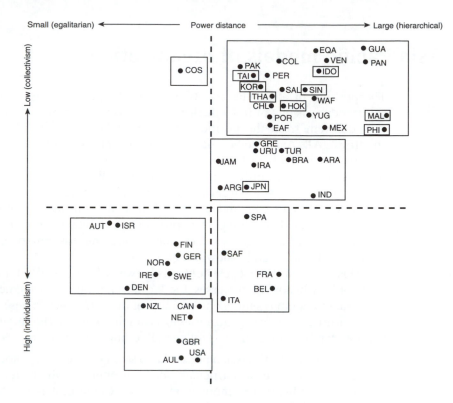

Figure 3.7   The core values of power distance and individualism/collectivism in different societies. (*Source*: Hofstede, 1984)

Key

ARA	Arab-speaking countries (Egypt, Lebanon, Lybia, Kuwait, Iraq, Saudi Arabia, United Arab Emirates)	
ARG	Argentina	
AUL	Australia	
AUT	Austria	
BEL	Belgium	
BRA	Brazil	
CAN	Canada	
CHL	Chile	
COL	Columbia	
COS	Costa Rica	
DEN	Denmark	
EAF	East Africa (Kenya, Ethiopia, Tanzania, Zambia)	
EQA	Equador	
FIN	Finland	

FRA	France
GBR	Great Britain
GER	West Germany (formerly)
GRE	Greece
GUA	Guatemala
HOK	Hong Kong
IDO	Indonesia
IND	India
IRA	Iran
IRE	Ireland (Republic of)
ISR	Israel
ITA	Italy
JAM	Jamaica
JPN	Japan
KOR	South Korea
MAL	Malaysia
MEX	Mexico
NET	Netherlands
NOR	Norway
NZL	New Zealand

PAK	Pakistan
PAN	Panama
PER	Peru
PHI	Philippines
POR	Portugal
SAF	South Africa
SAL	Salvador
SIN	Singapore
SPA	Spain
SWE	Sweden
TAI	Taiwan
THA	Thailand
TUR	Turkey
URU	Uruguay
USA	United States
VEN	Venezuela
WAF	West Africa (Nigeria, Ghana, Sierra Leone)
YUG	Yugoslavia (formerly)

Significantly, they mean that the psychological cement of many organizations within the Asia/Pacific region is paternalism. All of the five main types of organization found in the region, excluding the Western multi-national, are essentially paternalist in nature.

But why has paternalism evolved as the effective adaptation to the Asian context? In his study of social power structures in Asia, Lucian Pye of Massachusetts Institute of Technology (MIT) noted that: 'Power is extraordinarily sensitive to cultural nuances... More particularly, Asian cultures have historically had a rich variety of concepts of power. They share, however, the common denominator of idealizing benevolent, paternalistic leadership and of legitimizing dependency (high power distance).' There is also a tendency among Asians to suppress self-interest in favour of group solidarity, while anticipating welfare benefits in exchange for the loyalty and conformity offered (collectivism).

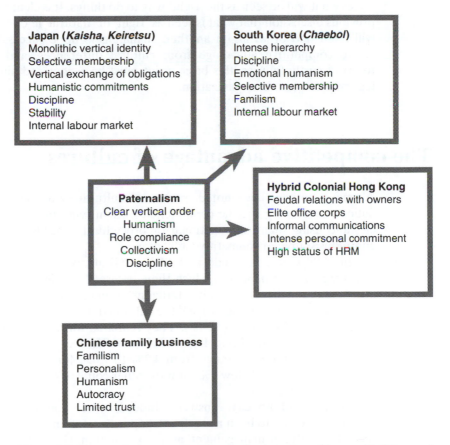

Figure 3.8 Four variations on the theme of paternalism. (*Source*: Redding and Baldwin, 1991)

Although the nature of the 'group' concerned may vary – in Japan it is usually the work group, for the Chinese inevitably the family – an organization that responds to the expectation of reciprocal assistance is accepted as legitimate and becomes psychologically comfortable for its members. The end result is a structure and order that is somehow 'natural', with an inherent discipline and conformity. The hierarchy is deemed legitimate (provided it is moral and benevolent) and cooperation is not a battleground. The subtleties of vertical obligation and rank may be invisible but they have a great deal to do with the internal efficiency of many Asian organizations (Redding and Baldwin, 1991).

The cultural origins of an organization's founders and leaders are important determinants of the strategies the firm will employ, how it will be organized, the qualities and capabilities that will be valued, and the characteristics of those who will rise to the top. Certainly industry, economic conditions, company size and other factors will influence the organization as well, but culture is pervasive and important as it determines what will be seen as the 'right' way to do things. It is clear from the previous discussion that what is seen as 'right' or 'natural' in one culture, will seem odd or wrong in another. If managers hope successfully to create competitive advantage from cultural differences, and indeed to avoid costly failures, this basic point must be recognized and made legitimate within the organization.

The competitive advantage of cultures

As many authors have noted, particular cultural values can lead to nations developing specific competencies. Identifying these competencies and using them for functional or procedural expertise can be an enormous source of competitive advantage.

In 1988 Geert Hofstede and Michael Bond wrote an article for *Organizational Dynamics* in which they discussed the link between the economic growth of 'The Five Dragons' (Singapore, Taiwan, South Korea, Hong Kong and Japan) and the cultural dimension of collectivism (*Organizational Dynamics*, 1988). They searched for an explanation of how, over a 21-year period from 1965 to 1985, average annual GNP growth per capita could range from 4.7% to 7.6% for these countries, while remaining well below 4% for most other countries during the same period (see Table 3.1).

They found no easy answers. Indeed, other countries such as Colombia seemed to be in a much better position for an economic takeoff in 1965. 'Better management' as an explanation, Hofstede and Bond argued, was too easy an answer because the quality of management

Table 3.1 Economic growth for selected countries and gross national product (GNP) per capita, 1965–85.

	1965–85 Average annual GNP/capita growth rate (%)	1965 GNP/capita US$ and rank	1985 GNP/capita US$ and rank
Singapore	7.6	550 (12)	7,420 (10)
Taiwan	7.2	220 (16)	3.600 (12)
South Korea	6.6	150 (17)	2,150 (13)
Hong Kong	6.1	590 (11)	6,230 (11)
Japan	4.7	780 (10)	11,300 (5)
Brazil	4.3	240 (15)	1,640 (15)
Austria	3.5	1,180 (8)	9,120 (8)
Colombia	2.9	280 (14)	1,320 (16)
Germany†	2.7	1,810 (5)	10,940 (6)
Canada	2.4	2,260 (3)	13,680 (3)
Netherlands	2.0	1,520 (7)	9,290 (7)
Sweden	1.8	2,160 (4)	11,890 (4)
India	1.7	90 (18)	270 (18)
USA	1.7	3,420 (1)	16,690 (1)
UK	1.6	1,580 (6)	8,460 (9)
Poland	1.5	840 (9)	2,050 (14)
Switzerland	1.4	2,310 (2)	16,370 (2)
Nicaragua	−2.1	330 (13)	770 (17)

Source: World Development Report 1987 and other statistics
†Excluding East Germany

depends on the qualities of the people to be managed. Also, 'the quality-of-management explanation', they wrote, 'begs the question of how an entire nation can collectively produce better management than another nation.' They proposed that culture was partly responsible, and that, in addition to the existence of a market and a political context that allows development, culture in the form of certain dominant values was also necessary for economic growth.

The shared culture of these societies, greater collectivism and Confucian roots, may have given them particular advantages in increasingly complex and dynamic markets. In addition, they noted, Eastern thinking is synthetic whereas Western thinking is analytical. Hofstede and Bond thus believe that the success of these societies in this period could be partially due to cultural preferences: 'What is true or who is right is less important than what works, and how the efforts of individuals with different thinking patterns can be coordinated toward a common goal.'

Michael Porter, in *The Competitive Advantage of Nations*, writes that 'national differences in character and culture, far from being threatened by global competition, prove integral to success in it' (Porter, 1990). In globally operating organizations, an emerging managerial challenge becomes identifying how particular cultures may offer advantages in terms of functional specialization (that is responsiveness), orientation to time (longer-term planning), technical capabilities, and so on. Organizations may then begin to establish 'centres of excellence' in different cultures where the orientation is better suited to the particular function or project.

In a recent thought-provoking book by Charles Hampden-Turner and Fons Trompenaars, the authors look at seven different cultures of capitalism – the USA, the UK, Japan, France, Germany, Sweden and the Netherlands – and examine how the particular values of each society have directed the different approaches each takes to achieve economic success (Hampden-Turner and Trompenaars, 1993). They explore the stereotypes that inform us that Germans are particularly good at building infrastructure and the Americans excel at invention (dreaming up new products), whereas the Japanese excel at innovation (getting those new products to market). They ask why such skills should correspond to nationality if wealth creation is the dry stuff of science and not the mysterious province of culture. One example from their premise that wealth creation is a moral act, its form determined by specific cultural values, is the USA's extraordinary economic successes, many of which can be attributed to the high value it places on both universalism and analysis.

> 'Examples of America's skilful application of universalist principles to business stretch from Henry Ford's Model T marketing promise: "You can have any color you like as long as it's black" to McDonald's and its near-identical foods and facilities available from Miami to Moscow. Even the fantasies of Walt Disney as featured in theme parks come in identical mechanized formats from Paris to Los Angeles. "It's a small world, after all…" The American ideal is of the Universal Product, reducible to parts (analysis) and infinitely replicable. We can see this in products as different as microprocessors and M&Ms, Coca-Cola and superconductors. What is aspired to is the widest possible product appeal (universalism) combined with a manufacturing process that is reduced to simple steps (analysis) so the parent company can manufacture wherever costs are lowest and sell to as many people as possible. It is the vision of the world's Cookie Cutter… The sheer extent of codification and preformulation in all aspects of American business sets it apart from the other cultures of capitalism.'

In Trompenaars's dimensions shown in Chapter 2, the USA is by far the most universalist culture in the study. No other culture is as keen to make rules for everyone to live by. And, as Hampden-Turner and Trompenaars write:

'No wonder, then, that the United States excelled early at mass manufacture and mass marketing. And should we be surprised that as markets became more customized, more fragmented, more oriented to unique requests, America's difficulties have mounted? This is especially true of competition with nations such as Japan and France which are culturally oriented to heterogeneity, variety and particularities – customized goods, haute cuisine and haute couture.'

Globally operating organizations are no longer able to be conditioned by the advantages or limitations of one cultural orientation nor should they wish to be. With an appreciation for the complexity and diversity of human cultures, it is possible to get the best from those who are best at it.

Siemens is one global company that had a relatively early start trying to build an understanding of cultural differences into the organization and to achieve advantages from realistic cultural synergies.

Case 3.5   Siemens

Siemens is a German world-class supplier of electrical and electronics products and systems. With operations in 132 countries, Siemens competes in power generation and transmission, telecommunications, medical engineering and semiconductors. The company employs over 400,000 people worldwide (250,000 Germans and 150,000 from other nationalities) and recorded 1991 sales of DM73 billion ($43 billion).

Vincent O'Neill, deputy director of Management Language and Intercultural Training at Siemens, explained that in the early 1980s senior management was sceptical of initial attempts to discuss strategies to manage cultural differences.

'Siemens is very bottom-line oriented. People are very sceptical of anything that doesn't have to do with results. So, any discussion about cultural differences had to be approached from the angle of how it would affect performance. In the early 1980s, after some problems with cross-border acquisitions, Siemens began to take the issue seriously. The approach to managing diversity which developed concentrated on international competitiveness. It is really about trying to achieve realistic cultural synergies and therefore about achieving better results.

continues

continued

'We have a two track approach. The long-term track is about development starting from apprentices all the way through to the Board – with a fairly strong focus on the younger group: apprentices, international project teams, transferees, and so on. The short-term track is project related. It focuses on the issue: how can people work together internationally in rapidly changing business situations? The need for this arises because of rapid changes from mergers, acquisitions, strategic alliances, and so on, which means that you have new constellations almost overnight. Your business can take on a radically different character and this poses enormous challenges to international managers who have to make major changes in complex business and cultural settings. So what do you do in those situations where you have to achieve a balance of cooperation and competitiveness, and still focus on the ultimate goal: the bottom line? It is not easily achieved, but it can be done.

'The concept involves three stages of training which are bracketed by those two tracks. The first stage is awareness. It sounds very simple but actually is one of the most difficult areas. It is getting people from a variety of national and business cultures to examine their own culture, the effects of their perception grid, their expectations, their value systems in communicating and working together internationally. We try to hold a mirror up, so to say, and have people realize that others do things differently and for good reasons. The second level is communication. Having realized that there are four key elements which have a strong influence on developments and therefore on business results – (1) my personal culture; (2) corporate culture and functional area culture; (3) the situation I am in; and (4) my "national" culture – people have to understand that those elements are all operating in all communication situations. And the question is, what has the critical influence in any particular business situation? Then we look at different situations and try to understand the role of each element. Each of the first three elements is affected by the fourth, by national culture.

'The third stage is introduced where there is a situation of crisis. This is where conflict has arisen and this is blocking the business and the results. The issue here is to try to come in with a process which involves clarification, both top down and bottom up, of what is happening in the situation; proposals as to how to change it across cultures in an international setting; and conflict management between the cultures involved. Again this is all done with the aim of turning the situation around and producing results in business terms.'

continues

continued

> In Mr O'Neill's view, the formation of a culture which is able to gain competitive advantage from cultural differences must be regarded as a continuous process that involves tensions. It is not a strategy that can be considered finalised and written in tablets of stone. It is an ongoing process in the long- and short-term and must always be open to development and change.

In fact, many companies have made a commitment to internationalizing at a strategic level. The following are examples of the mechanisms that companies like Siemens, ABB, Honeywell and many others are using to become more representative of the markets in which they operate:

- Making boards of directors more international.
- Holding international meetings where people share information (that is, technical, functional, projects).
- Forming multicultural teams or task forces.
- Increasing the number of foreigners in headquarters.
- Rotating staff across cultures.
- Attempting to 'share best practice'.

While these are important and valid steps, they often remain at the level of coexistence. In other words, many organizations find that the meeting of two or more cultures does not in itself add value. Some of the obstacles that typically get in the way with cultural learning are summarized below.

Box 3.1   Cultural learning disabilities

- *I am my national culture.* In an intercultural encounter, people tend to define their personal identity by referring to their national identity. They seek the fundamental values and norms that define their society to decide how they should behave in dealing with people from different cultures. They then overvalue their own culture and adopt an ethnocentric attitude.

continues

continued

- *People from a different culture are my enemies.* In dealing with people from other cultures, people tend to assume that the others will try to impose their values. They may become transformed into a warrior, a defender of their national honour, with the attitude 'I will not let them get away with it!'. This is usually the result of feeling threatened and insecure in the interaction with another culture.
- *The illusion that 'I am helping them develop'.* Those who consider their own ways to be better or more sophisticated than those of another culture can focus on the view 'I will teach them my ways so that they can become more advanced'. They take on the role of 'conqueror, expert, missionary or educator'.
- *The illusion that 'I have the answer'.* Since people adopt the role of the 'expert' or 'teacher', they tend to transfer the techniques that have worked so well 'back home'. They usually assume that they know what is best for the other culture in the long run. This is usually done without realizing that pushing for a solution that works well in one culture can often have negative consequences elsewhere.
- *The delusion of being able to understand another culture just by living there.* Often people believe that, just because they have learned to live or work successfully in another culture, they understand it completely. But often a great deal more time is spent criticizing the other culture than is taken to understand why people from another culture do what they do.
- *The myth of the expert.* There is often the belief that, if only the visitor has enough technical expertise, cultural expertise is not necessary. A supplementary assumption can prevail with some technical experts that they can easily become a cultural expert since, after all, 'the soft stuff is easier to understand than the hard stuff'.

A model of cultural learning

In order for organizations to use cultural differences competitively, it is certainly important for the assumptions about the role of culture to change. The people at the top of the organization must recognize both the potential benefits and the problems that culture can create. The steps outlined above are important and necessary in developing a strategy to manage across cultures. However, cultural learning at an operational level should be considered a strategic requirement.

At the practical level of managing across cultures, the companies that have been successfully translating 'cultural synergy' into action seem to be using four important steps in specific cultural encounters:

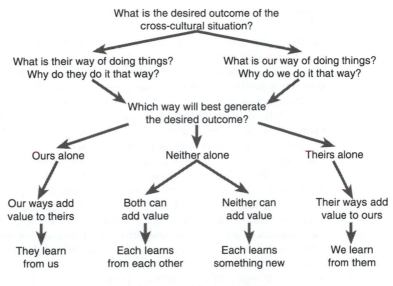

Figure 3.9   A model of cultural learning.

(1)   A very considered process of making implicit knowledge explicit.
(2)   Agreeing on the specific outcomes that are desired from the inter-
      action.
(3)   Understanding why each culture does things the way it does and
      agreeing which approach or combination of approaches will lead to
      achieving the desired outcomes.
(4)   Reviewing the outcomes and modifying the approach to fit both
      cultures and the desired outcomes better.

The 'decision-tree' in Figure 3.9 illustrates the process that the
following case studies of cultural learning describe.

Case 3.6   *Cultural learning at Toshiba in the UK*

When Toshiba gained 100% ownership of the former 70:30
Rank–Toshiba joint venture in Plymouth, UK, in 1981, the process of
cultural learning started immediately. The management process that

continues

continued

Toshiba went through involved understanding that the British were used to one way of working and the Japanese to another, and that the way to achieve its objectives would sometimes be the Japanese way, sometimes the British way and sometimes a hybrid of the two.

Dennis Swadling, then the production director at Plymouth, had been with Rank for several years. He saw the operation through the formation of the joint venture and negotiated and implemented the new practices, policies and culture as Toshiba took it over and turned it into a quality award-winning, high-profile symbol of manufacturing success in the UK. He explained the process of making it work. 'Right up front we evaluated as many policies as we could think through.' It was a lengthy and detailed process. 'Every aspect of the business was discussed, the desired outcomes were agreed and the ways to make them happen.' There were not only financial objectives, but also objectives aimed at developing a particular company culture. For each aim, a team of Japanese and English managers discussed every detail and worked through them together. They discussed their different approaches and negotiated the most effective way of ensuring the desired outcome. During the whole process of reviewing policies and practices, 'we jointly determined we were trying to strike a balance between having concern for people and still being a hard task master'.

The level of detail in the points listed below shows the importance the team placed on a coherent set of practices that would achieve the 'team spirit/equal status' objective. For each of these 16 points, both sides' cultural preferences were considered. As the team reviewed each desired outcome, the British managers' knowledge of the methods and style of communication that should be used, the level of information to be conveyed and the things that would motivate or demotivate the British workforce were combined with the Japanese managers' practical experience in manufacturing televisions (see Figure 3.10).

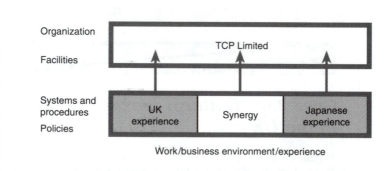

Work/business environment/experience

Figure 3.10 Toshiba consumer products operating philosophy (blended). (*Source*: Toshiba Consumer Products Ltd)

continues

continued

Actions to develop a 'team spirit/equal status' industrial culture

(1)   Careful selection and induction of staff
(2)   Autonomy of local management
(3)   Open style of management and consultation
(4)   Five-minute morning meetings, monthly meetings, six-monthly business reviews
(5)   Few levels of management
(6)   Open-plan offices
(7)   Development of a team approach
(8)   All staff with common terms and conditions
(9)   Uniform work clothes
(10) Grade promotional opportunities
(11) Attendance and timekeeping disciplines
(12) No smoking or food in production areas
(13) Individual responsibility for space cleaning
(14) Emphasis on localized teams
(15) Formal annual performance review and defined improvement/ supportive training
(16) Single-status restaurant

One critical element in the company's production system is for all team members to do the same job, the same way, every time. If they have an idea for a way to change what they do, they must not execute it, but rather go through a very involved process of discussing it and considering the impact the change might have on all other aspects of the system. The Japanese and British members of the management team understood and agreed that this was the right way of working, but recognized that the English culture was more attuned to individual performance and showing initiative within an individual's own area of responsibility. The management had to explain clearly why the consensual Japanese way of working was required and the implications for all the other team members if someone initiated a change that did not work.

Neil Lancaster, senior production manager, explained that, after having worked for a US machining company, he found this a new way of working. Although he understood the rationale, it took time to adjust to this counter-cultural way of working: 'I was used to getting on and doing the job if you think it needs doing. It was frustrating at first.' But eventually he and his colleagues realized the importance of this approach. The Managing Director of the operation, George Williams, is British and had had experience working for American and German consumer products companies previously. He explained his perspective on developing cultural synergies.

continues

---

continued

> 'Nationality really does not matter. You just accept people as international business people. This is a very consultative, communicative company. We try to blend the best of both cultures... you must recognize that every culture has something to offer. The point is to respect each culture and try to understand it. If you can say, "We bring this, this and this – you bring that; help us understand it." That's ideal.'

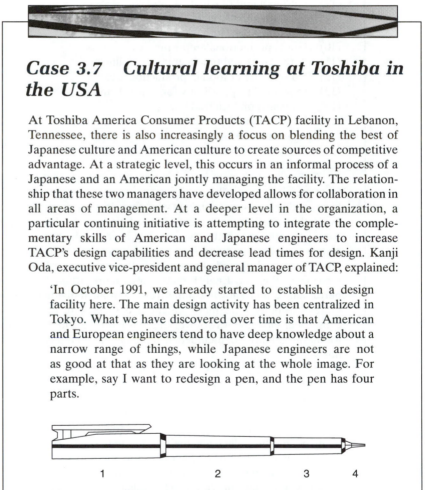

Case 3.7   Cultural learning at Toshiba in the USA

At Toshiba America Consumer Products (TACP) facility in Lebanon, Tennessee, there is also increasingly a focus on blending the best of Japanese culture and American culture to create sources of competitive advantage. At a strategic level, this occurs in an informal process of a Japanese and an American jointly managing the facility. The relationship that these two managers have developed allows for collaboration in all areas of management. At a deeper level in the organization, a particular continuing initiative is attempting to integrate the complementary skills of American and Japanese engineers to increase TACP's design capabilities and decrease lead times for design. Kanji Oda, executive vice-president and general manager of TACP, explained:

> 'In October 1991, we already started to establish a design facility here. The main design activity has been centralized in Tokyo. What we have discovered over time is that American and European engineers tend to have deep knowledge about a narrow range of things, while Japanese engineers are not as good at that as they are looking at the whole image. For example, say I want to redesign a pen, and the pen has four parts.

1	2	3	4

> The more complicated parts, (1) and (4), could be designed by American engineers in Tennessee. The more standardized parts (2) and (3) could be designed by Japanese engineers in

continues

continued

Fukaya [Toshiba's Consumer Products facility in Japan]. Fukaya engineers could also be responsible for the total design integration. With this capability, using the special skills of American design engineers, we can adapt more closely to what the local market prefers. Also, we could have shorter lead times in the different markets where we are able to do this.'

The cultural assumptions that help explain these differing strengths and ways of solving problems have to do with the more specific ways of thinking characteristic of Americans and northern Europeans compared with the more synthetic, diffuse approaches of Japanese and Latin cultures.

American	*Japanese*
Analytical thinking	Synthetic thinking
Specific	Relational
Reduce problems into parts	Holistic, integrative approach

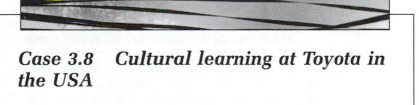

Step-by-step approach to problem-solving	Holistic approach to problem solving

By combining these two approaches for different engineering requirements, Toshiba is attempting to build competitive advantage at a concrete, operational level.

Case 3.8   *Cultural learning at Toyota in the USA*

Toyota's first wholly owned manufacturing operation in the USA started production in 1988 in Georgetown, Kentucky. Transferring specific ways of doing business at Toyota, especially its highly successful and often reviewed Toyota Production System (TPS), was not just a matter of teaching the 'techniques' to new American employees. The process involved identifying basic cultural assumptions behind Toyota's management and production philosophies, understanding relevant aspects of American culture, and trying to integrate the two. Fujio Cho,

continues

continued

president and chief executive officer of Toyota Motor Manufacturing USA, explained the process at a strategic level.

Some of the critical requirements in Toyota's way of operating in Japan required employees' involvement in the key areas of:

- Taking an active role in quality control.
- Using employee ideas and opinions in the production process.
- Participating in '*Kaizen*', which is the constant striving for improvement.

Furthermore, Toyota 'team members', the term used for all employees, are expected to treat the next employee on the production line as their customer and are not to pass a defective part on to that employee. If a problem is found with a part of the automobile, the team member is expected to stop the line and the source of the problem is examined and corrected. This Toyota philosophy is called '*Jidoka*'.

Mr Cho, who was instrumental in developing the company's production system in the mid-1970s, explained the basic philosophy behind the Toyota Production System. 'The most important thing is that you can find a variety of waste in the production process and you try to eliminate the waste. It is a whole philosophy, in which everyone is participating. Because of this it is definitely important to motivate people not just in our plant, but also suppliers.'

Some of the key differences in work-related cultural assumptions and practices between Toyota's Japanese and American workforces are listed in Table 3.2.

Mr Cho explained the process Toyota went through in bringing its manufacturing to the USA.

'When we came to the United States, we re-examined what we had been doing every day in Japan. We had to think about the implications of the way we were used to doing things. The first thought I had was, although there are differences in culture, to focus on the basic bottom line of being human beings... so we could deal with the similarities. For example, if someone tells you "You don't have to think, just do what I tell you", most Japanese people would get mad. So would most other people. It may sound rather simplistic, but my conclusion from what I have experienced is that you should not lose sight of the basic things.'

The basic things that Mr Cho used as the shared culture with Toyota in Japan were behaviours rather than simply statements:

- Treat human beings with respect and as the most important aspect of the business.
- Nurture people in their profession.
- Emphasize the importance of the people on the shop floor.
- Do what you say you are going to do... build trust.

continues

continued

Table 3.2   Different cultural assumptions.

Aspects of management:	American	Japanese
Boss–subordinate relationship	Subordinates given specific responsibilities	Subordinates given broad responsibilities
	Subordinates need decisions from supervisors	Consensus on group goals
Loyalty	Low degree demanded by company	High degree demanded by company
Rewards	Short-term; based on performance	Long-term; based on seniority
Functional knowledge	Specialists	Generalists
Job descriptions	Need details of individual job	Broad guidelines of group's goals
Cultural assumptions:	Individualism	Collectivism
	Contractual relations (Universalistic)	Relations based on inter-personal trust (Particularist)
	Value formal credentials	Value experience
	Specialization	Integration (synthetic thinking)
	Short-term orientation	Long-term orientation

Nate Furuta, a senior human resource executive now at the Georgetown facility, was instrumental in the integration of the GM–Toyota 'NUMMI' joint venture in California. He described what he believes are the most critical elements of building from what each culture has to offer.

'If you understand the logic of another culture, then you can find points of connection to work with and you can be success-ful. You need to look at why people do what they do. That's a very basic concept in my mind. If I understand why people do it their way, then I can come up with a solution.'

Mr Furuta described some very practical examples of the implica-tions of cultural differences at the operational level. Essentially, turning would-be problems into understanding and eventually into learning means that you have to explain why each culture does what it does.

'When a Japanese manager feels uncomfortable with people calling him by his first name, I have to explain both sides. Why is he uncomfortable? Japanese are very conscious of hierarchy. We have been taught that you must respect someone with experience. So, if we don't know each other at all and don't

continues

continued

know who is higher ranking or lower ranking, the simple way is you must respect whoever is older. That is why we exchange business cards so frequently. You get the card and you think "Oh, this person is president of such and such. How does that relate to my position?" Then you change your language. There are polite words and frank words. You have to determine whether very polite language is required. If a Japanese boss comes to the USA and he is called by his first name, in Japan that would be very impolite. So I have to explain this.

'If you have the essence of why Japanese do it one way, or Americans do it one way, then you can find a way to get the outcome you want.'

For example, it is very important in the Toyota Production System, accepted across all areas of the business, that people have shared responsibility so that things do not fall through the cracks created when everyone has distinct and separate responsibilities. To achieve this in Japan, Toyota provides broad job descriptions and rotates people much more frequently than is customary in the USA. This practice has many implications:

- People gain broad experience of different aspects of the organization.
- Today's boss or subordinate will probably not be so next year or at least not in five years.
- It enables the sharing of information and personal development because responsibility is taken by the group.

'We discovered that responsibility in the USA means one's "territory". They think, "This is my responsibility, don't touch on my responsibilities." There can be differences in understanding what that means. The Japanese way is that someone might have many responsibilities, but group responsibilities prevail. This allows individuals to discuss what they are doing and how things are going. If they have a problem, they can ask for help – without it being an insult. But if Americans are given certain responsibilities, they may feel that if they ask for help it will be interpreted as their being incompetent. So here, you often find that people don't want to share information so they can keep their own territory. They may also feel that if they develop their people, they may lose their job because then their subordinate may be able to do their job and they would no longer be needed.

'Once we understand the logical reasons why people from this culture don't want to share information, we can see if together we can find ways to get the outcomes we want.'

continues

continued

All of the managers agreed that the desired outcomes of no defects and no gaps in responsibilities would best be accomplished if people shared information, had joint responsibility and developed their peers and subordinates. They found new ways of working together that could help lead to these outcomes. A large part of the strategy was to build trust between management and employees, which they recognized would take a long time. In the shorter term, they developed reward systems and promotion policies that rewarded behaviours that were derived from the implicit cultural assumptions of the Japanese workforce.

'We emphasize job security. We stress that if you develop people, then you will be promoted. If you don't, you can't be promoted because there wouldn't be anyone to replace you. They must teach their people. That is also what they are evaluated against. But the important thing is that you need to take out the fear and ensure that no one is terminated (made redundant) for developing people, rather to reward people for it. There's a logical reason why people would not want to share information, or risk developing their people. Again, it comes down to knowing why both sides do what they do.'

A value-added perspective on managing across cultures

The ways in which companies are adding value with culture seem to involve a very proactive approach at an operational level. Managers from each culture must jointly work through the following steps.

- What is the desired outcome?
- What is each culture's way of doing things?
- Why do we do it that way?
- Which way will lead to the desired outcome?
- Agree to an approach or create new alternatives, blending approaches.
- Implement solution(s) and review the impact from a joint perspective.
- Refine the solution based on multicultural feedback.

The process should be seen as a continuing refinement of understanding and as generating new solutions rather than as an isolated event to solve a particular problem.

Summary

Evolving organizational structures and competitive requirements demand that managers in globally competitive organizations change their assumptions about the impact of cultural differences. They also require a more proactive strategy for managing across cultures. The strategies that have been employed as firms have moved from being multidomestic to being international and multinational are not sophisticated enough to allow for differences in national culture to be used competitively.

While some firms are taking the necessary steps towards managing cultural differences strategically, they must move beyond tolerance and cooperation and begin to build cultural synergies at an operational level. This does appear to be occurring in some organizations. The more common approach currently being adopted seems to include at least five steps for a particular cross-cultural issue. These include:

(1) Jointly determining the desired outcome.
(2) Articulating each culture's way of doing things and explicitly describing why it is done that way.
(3) Determining which approach will best generate the desired outcome and, if neither will alone, generating new alternatives.
(4) Implementing the approach.
(5) Modifying with multicultural feedback.

The process seems to be a continuing, evolving process rather than a discrete event.

However, the one risk always to bear in mind is that if one culture dominates another, then a prime advantage of multinationalism will be lost. There is no one best way, not even a best way of finding the best way. The cases where successful companies have sought to explain how they manage national diversity all show a natural and irreducible component of ethnocentrism. Ikea is uncompromisingly Swedish, Emerson explicitly American, Toshiba unapologetically Japanese and Seimens thoroughly German. Perhaps the truly global company is still a generation away. Perhaps it cannot be originated in a country which is so economically dominant as to encourage the arrogance of colonialists.

It is encouraging, however, that more and more organizations are appreciating the need, and there is an increasing awareness of the means by which international diversity can be positioned to provide competitive advantage.

References

Adler N.J. (1983). Organizational development in a multicultural environment. *Journal of Applied Behavioural Science*, **19**(3), 249–365

Adler N.J. (1986). *International Dimensions of Organizational Behavior.* Boston, MA: Kent Publishing Co

Adler N.J., Doktor R. and Redding G.S. (1986). From the Atlantic to the Pacific century: cross-cultural management reviewed. In *Yearly Review of Management of the Journal of Management* Hunt J.G. and Blair J.D., eds., **12**, 295–318

Barnham K. and Devine M. (1993). *The Quest for the International Manager: A Survey of Global Human Resource Strategies.* London: The Economist Intelligence Unit

Hampden-Turner C. and Trompenaars F. (1993). *The Seven Cultures of Capitalism: Value Systems for Creating Wealth in the United States, Britain, Japan, Germany, France, Sweden, and the Netherlands.* New York: Doubleday

Hofstede G. (1984). *Culture's Consequences: International Differences in Work-Related Values.* Beverley Hills, California: Sage Publications

Hofstede G. (1991). *Cultures and Organizations: Software of the Mind.* London: McGraw-Hill

Hofstede G. and Bond M.H. (1988). The Confucius connection: from cultural roots to economic growth. *Organizational Dynamics*, **16**(4), 4–21

Knight C.F. (1992). HBR case study: Emerson Electric. *Harvard Business Review*, January/February

Kotter J.P. and Heskett J.L. (1992). *Corporate Culture and Performance.* New York: The Free Press

Porter M.E. (1990). *The Competitive Advantage of Nations.* New York: The Free Press

Redding S.G. and Baldwin E. (1991). *Managers for Asia/Pacific: Recruitment and Development Strategies.* Hong Kong: Business International

4

Advertising across cultures

Do 'global' products exist?

The lowering of economic barriers across Europe and within North America and Mexico, as well as evolving trade relationships in the Far East, have hastened marketers' continuing search for ways to rationalize product lines and harmonize marketing activities internationally. While there is still mention of so-called 'global' products marketed with 'global' messages to increasingly homogeneous consumers, their potential in this sense is very limited. Marketing across cultures is a complex process of balancing resources and effectiveness between building product strength and identity on the one hand and increasing geographical coverage on the other (Gogel and Larreche, 1991). Culture plays a very important role in striking the right balance.

The impact of cultural differences has long been recognized by marketers in multinational organizations. Owing to early and costly lessons (see Box 4.1), marketing is probably the functional area most accustomed to considering culture in international business. Moreover, the ways in which marketing and advertising executives are taking culture into account are necessarily becoming more sophisticated as markets globalize. Rather than simply considering language and behavioural differences, there is increasingly an attempt to understand the meanings that consumers in different cultures give to products, brands, messages and behaviours. Even the ways that advertising agencies conduct 'lifestyle' research and other forms of market segmentation more and more include allowances for how culture directs and influences the differing ways consumers perceive products and services.

Box 4.1   Critical lessons from early international marketing experiences

Inappropriate translations

Many of the largest consumer goods companies learned early lessons about marketing across cultures. The most common problems were, and in many cases still are, the literal translations of brand names or slogans into other languages. Pillsbury's Jolly Green Giant brand, for example, was translated literally as 'Intimidating Green Ogre' in Saudi Arabia. And General Motors introduced the Chevy NOVA in Mexico only to find out later that *no va* in Spanish means does not go! In Latin America, a product had to be taken off the market when the manufacturer found that the name, when translated into the local language, meant 'Jackass oil'. When Kentucky Fried Chicken used its famous slogan "It's finger-licking good!" in Iran, it came out as "It's so good you will eat your fingers!" in Farsi.

Translation is the most basic level at which international marketing must adapt to cultural differences. The next level of learning comes from hard lessons on adapting products to differing cultural behaviours, physiques and ways of using products.

Different cultural behaviours and product usage

Procter & Gamble created the market for disposable nappies in Japan when it entered with Pampers in 1978. The product was the same nappy sold on the American market. P & G captured 10% of the market for nappies and had no competition in disposables. Japanese companies seized the opportunity, though, and began to produce disposable nappies that were more appropriate for Japanese consumers. The nappy for the American market was thick and bulky, designed to leave on babies for longer than Japanese mothers would leave a nappy on their babies. Competitors introduced thinner, more absorbent nappies in compact packaging designed for the smaller accommodation of Japanese households. They used super-absorbent polymers and priced their product at a premium. Pampers was almost driven out of the market.

continues

> *continued*
>
> P & G reacted quickly, though, and is still learning to adapt. Richard Laube, at that time the Swiss-born Pampers brand manager in Japan, explained in 1987:
>
> 'To survive and rebuild the business in Japan, Pampers has had to upgrade its product no less than four times in the last 36 months. This Pamper is now three times thinner than the original model. It is shaped for a better fit on Japanese babies, has a waist shield, and leg gathers to stop leaks. It has thick guidelines and refastenable tapes for convenience. It is now the best diaper in Japan. It allowed P & G to go from a 7% market share to 28% with market leadership in 30 months.' (Artzt, 1987)
>
> The lessons P & G learned in Japan have led to more competitive products in other markets. Thinner, better fitting Pampers are now also available in other national markets.

While culture certainly affects industrial marketing, it generally does so in a more indirect way. In other words, product standards and specifications may need to change to meet market-specific requirements, which may differ *because* of culture. The purchase and use of industrial goods, however, tend to be more standardized than those of consumer goods. Therefore, the focus here will be on how organizations which are advertising and marketing consumer goods across cultures are balancing the search for products with geographical coverage with the need to adapt to local differences in culture.

Global products, global meanings?

The internationalization of many forms of explicit culture (for example, dress, music, language) has been accelerated by electronic communication. Several consumer goods companies seem to have successfully extended certain products and services into international markets by capitalizing on images created by a worldwide communications network.

Levi Strauss jeans, for example, are the same product everywhere they are sold, although their meaning may differ. Indeed, many products and services are becoming common to global markets and the search is on for more. However, marketers and advertisers that are looking at a global marketplace are increasingly considering not simply what products and brands are to be found where, but *what they mean to the people in each culture*. If the intended meaning or image of the product, brand or service is not the same as the meaning perceived by the consumer, both the local brand strength and the benefits of geographical coverage are compromised.

The potential for global products

Few would agree with Theodore Levitt's infamous stance in the *Harvard Business Review* article, 'The globalization of markets' (1983).

> 'Different cultural preferences, national tastes and stan-
> dards, and business institutions are vestiges of the past... The
> world's needs and desires have been irrevocably homogen-
> ized. This makes the multinational corporation obsolete and
> the global corporation absolute... Instead of adapting to
> superficial and even entrenched differences within and
> between nations, the global corporation will seek sensibly to
> force suitably standardized products and practices on the
> entire globe.'

Though there are differing views on global marketing (see Box 4.2), most scholars and practitioners agree that harmonization, not standard-ization, is the necessary response to global markets.

The potential for global products indeed seems small. Even for products that seem purely functional and free of cultural expectations there are differences in how they are perceived across cultures. Research conducted by Colgate-Palmolive, for example, found that toothpaste is viewed as a cosmetic product in Spain and Greece, but is seen in the Netherlands as more of a treatment to prevent cavities. Similarly, Spaniards treat soap as a cosmetic item, while the British consider it a functional commodity (Business International, 1990). Food and beverage products are notoriously difficult to standardize. Instant coffee, for example, is less popular in Germany, France, Italy and the

Box 4.2   Views on global marketing

Michael Porter

Is Ted Levitt right about the globalization of markets? Yes. Does that mean that you standardize and homogenize the way you perform marketing in every country in the world throughout the marketing mix? Of course not. (Porter, 1992)

Kenichi Ohmae

When it comes to product strategy, managing in a borderless world doesn't mean managing by averages. It doesn't mean that all tastes run together into one amorphous mass of universal appeal. And it doesn't mean that the appeal of operating globally removes the obligation to localize products. The lure of a universal product is a false allure. The truth is a bit more subtle... Managing effectively in this new borderless environment means paying attention to delivering value to customers – and to developing an equidistant view of who they are and what they want. Before everything else comes the need to see your customers clearly. They – and only they – can provide legitimate reasons for thinking global. (Ohmae, 1989)

J. Krielen, commercial director, Nestlé

Being a truly global company means being an insider in the major markets around the world.

J. W. Eenhoorn, group executive (Ice Cream and Sweet Snacks), Unilever

Unilever in most of its product groups still adheres to the adage 'think global, act local'. Of course we are re-evaluating our current portfolio with a view towards harmonization. And we feel that our core brands should all have an international dimension. But, to enable a flexible response to market trends, still a lot has to be done locally. Unilever still uses the local market as its power base. For products with international potential, we have central guidelines as to how they should be marketed. However, local managers can still make modifications if they are consumer-relevant.

Marco Rivetti, chairman, Gruppo GFT

For GFT, globalization is not about standardization, it's about a quantum increase in complexity. The more the company has penetrated global markets, the more sustaining its growth depends on responding to the myriad of local differences in its key markets around the world. To be global means to recognize differences and be flexible enough to adapt to them. (*Harvard Business Review*, 1991)

Netherlands, where people have deeply rooted traditions of coffee drinking and want it freshly brewed, while it is more popular in countries like the UK, Ireland and the USA. When the British talk about coffee, they in fact mean instant coffee unless it is referred to explicitly as 'filter coffee'. Furthermore, products with long-standing usage habits are difficult to market internationally. Cheese is an example of a popular food in many cultures, whose usage varies greatly across cultures. In France it is eaten after dinner, before dessert; in the Netherlands it is eaten with breakfast; while the British and Americans tend to eat it at lunch time.

Products that have been successful across cultures seem to fall into two categories. Those at the 'high' end of the market – for example, Prêt à Porter clothing, Hennessey brandy, Moët & Chandon champagne, Porsche cars, classical music and the *Financial Times* – appeal to consumers with similar lifestyles and expectations regardless of culture. At the 'low' end, there are also products that seem able to cross cultural boundaries unchanged – Coca-Cola soft drinks, McDonald's restaurants, Levi's jeans, pop music, personal stereos and ice cream bars. 'Low' end does not imply lower quality. Rather, these products are usually targeted at younger people, are impulse purchases and/or are novel products for which there are no pre-existing expectations. In the main, however, most consumer products fall somewhere in between, where cultural and product expectations do, in fact, already exist. Figure 4.1 shows how it is more important to adapt the advertising message for consumer business than it is for industrial business; it also illustrates how advertising must be increasingly adapted as the number of cultural perceptions viewing the message grows.

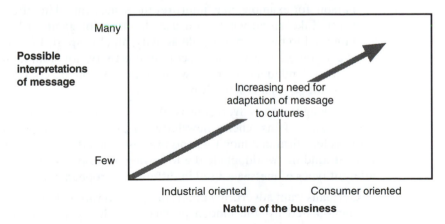

Figure 4.1   Adapting advertising messages for different cultures.

The potential for global messages

Jim Williams, director of strategy and method for Europe of the US advertising agency Young & Rubicam (Y&R), explained that, in his opinion, there is little scope for standardizing advertising across cultures: 'Complete standardization in communication will not happen, except in a very few instances, and where you would accept a very small market share everywhere, for example with a niche brand.' He gave several reasons for this belief.

> 'There are differences in the styles of communication that are effective and acceptable in different cultures, for example between high-context and low-context cultures. Americans are a low-context culture; they generally start from the assumption that the listener knows nothing. The French, on the other hand, are a high-context culture. They start from the assumption that the listener knows everything. What tends to happen is that the French will think the Americans *think* they are stupid because they start explaining everything, and vice versa.'

Mr Williams further explained:

> 'The degree of sentimentality people can stand varies enormously across cultures. A Kodak ad selling on "memories" that might work very well in the USA, could be terrible in the UK. If the product were targeted as a "hobby", emphasizing technical features, you would not need as much adaptation. But as soon as you add an emotional dimension, you need to be very aware of cultural differences.
>
> 'Finally, you have to be careful with your target audience. They may look different in different cultures; a status-conscious person, for example, may interpret the same symbol in different ways. Take an ad where you use shooting (of game or birds) intended to be a very up-scale activity, an elite sport. In Italy, it is considered a very average, common activity, not at all related to the intended meaning. So what you think you are conveying, may not be what is actually perceived.'

The language of advertising is also different across cultures. In a recent issue of its client newsletter *Topline*, McCollum/Spielman Worldwide, a firm that monitors and pre-tests the effectiveness of advertising around the world, made the following general observations about different types of messages used in different European markets:

- Germans want advertising that is factual and rational: they fear being manipulated by 'the hidden persuader'. The typical German spot features the standard family of two parents, two children and the grandmother.

- The French avoid reasoning or logic. Their advertising is predominantly emotional, dramatic and symbolic. Spots are viewed as cultural events – art for the sake of money – and are reviewed as if they were literature or films.
- The British value laughter above all else. The typical broad, self-deprecating British commercial amuses by mocking both the advertiser and the consumer.

The firm has found that in all European countries, and most particularly in Eastern Europe (where advertising has now become a fact of everyday life), 40% of those questioned in its surveys partly or completely failed to understand commercials (*Market-Europe*, 1993).

Leo van Os, international client director of one of the top 10 worldwide advertising agencies, Lintas, believes it is, indeed, *possible* to 'de-culturize' the setting of advertisements and make them more universal, but probably not preferable.

> 'Of course we can do that, but then you lose part of your strength, you "de-optimize". It is thinking with the wrong frame of mind, settling for something less attractive to consumers because it reduces costs. This is anti-marketing.'

Mr van Os explained that it is dangerous to talk about 'global' marketing because advertising should appeal to the *individual*.

> 'The rationale for globalizing should be getting better commercials in as many countries as relevant and as quickly as possible. It should be a quest for optimal effectiveness instead of just efficiency. Global marketing should be more about value, not primarily cost. Consumers do not deliberately buy a global product. It is not their concern to know if a brand is available elsewhere in the world. Consumers are prepared to pay a price for what is focused individually at them. They make individual choices. Marketing is about satisfying individual needs; that includes global marketing.'

In fact, many marketers and advertisers are trying to reckon with this very trend: there seems to be an increasing desire on the part of consumers for individuation of messages. 'Consumers want to be approached as individuals,' van Os explained. Mr Williams, too, pointed to this 'important value trend' as contradicting the business trend towards cost-saving rationalization and standardization (see Figure 4.2). He sees this desire for individuation as driving behaviour further apart.

The ways in which many internationally operating organizations seem to be balancing the need to build brand strength effectively and at the same time increasing geographical coverage have to do with managing the *meaning* of brands across cultures. This is, in a sense, a higher

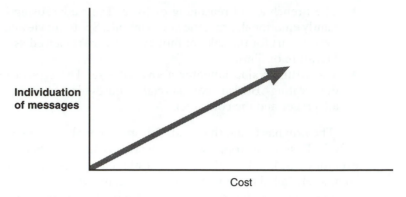

Individuation
of messages

Cost

Figure 4.2   Individuation of messages contradicts cost-saving rationalization.

level of sophistication in adapting to cultural differences than language
or cultural variations in product usage. The focus seems to be more and
more on ensuring that the intended meaning of the brand coincides with
the perceived meaning of the message (see Figure 4.3).

In order to achieve effective communication, the intended meaning
of product brands and the perceived meanings that consumers from
different cultures give to them must coincide. However, as discussed in
Chapter 2 and the previous section, differences in culture determine the
effectiveness of how and what is perceived. So how can the match
between intended meaning and perceived meaning occur most cost

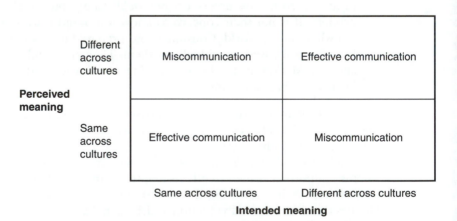

Perceived
meaning

	Different across cultures	Miscommunication	Effective communication
Perceived meaning	Same across cultures	Effective communication	Miscommunication
		Same across cultures	Different across cultures

Intended meaning

Figure 4.3   The intended meaning of the brand should coincide with the
perceived meaning of the message.

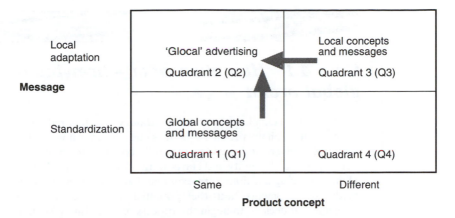

Figure 4.4   The managing meaning matrix.

effectively? The answer is to standardize the product or service *concept* globally, but allow for local adaptation of the message (see Figure 4.4).

Same product concept: standardization of advertising

Obviously, the greatest economies of scale and cost savings in marketing and advertising would fall in the Quadrant 1 category in Figure 4.4. Truly global products and services would be in this quadrant. The scope for success with this strategy, however, seems very limited.

As in the Heineken case study, values often thought to be universal may, in fact, be a reflection of the cultural context in which they are being considered. The value trend Heineken thought to be universal, that is a shift towards authenticity, simplicity and honesty, is, not surprisingly, a *Dutch* one. This is a very important and costly assumption to consider. As with any research, identifying 'universal' trends cannot escape the researcher's own assumptions and ways of seeing the world. It is simply not realistic for people to 'set aside' their cultural lenses to look for trends that are 'out there' to be discovered. Such trends are about similarities in people's ways of interpreting events, products, relationships, and so on. Culture provides a vehicle for trying to make sense of what is behind something that on the surface may appear to be a trend.

Case 4.1 Heineken beer – brewing a global brand

In the 1980s, Heineken's marketing strategy was tailored to foreign locales. Although the product was the same wherever it was sold in the world, the advertising message differed according to local consumer behaviour, brand identity and cultural tradition. In the 1990s, however, Heineken thought it time to re-examine that strategy in the context of media developments and the potential emergence of a 'Euro-consumer'. It decided to begin the process of establishing Heineken as a global brand: not only the same product but also the same message throughout Europe. The first step was the introduction of a European advertising theme. A European Brand Team was formed which would be responsible for the design and execution of the campaign across national boundaries.

The team based the advertising theme on the assumption that, even though individual tastes may differ, as long as quality is guaranteed and the advertising messages provoke the same 'universal' tastes and feelings, they could succeed with a global product. The idea for the 'universal' image grew out of what the team saw as a value trend across Europe. The trend they identified was that values were shifting away from pretentiousness towards more 'authentic', 'pure', yet sophisticated behaviour.

The advertising idea

The goal of the advertising idea that came out of the universal brand concept was to create a 'Heineken moment'. The television advertising messages focused on the transition from a stressful situation to relaxation, with Heineken. One of the commercials shows a young woman getting ready to go out with her friend. She stands in front of her wardrobe and is desperately looking for a dress to put on for a formal evening out. Her male friend, already dressed in a dinner jacket, is looking at her. He is obviously amused by her distress. He leaves the room and comes back dressed in casual clothing – jeans and a leather jacket. He hands her a pair of her own jeans. The pressure is off, and so is the plan for the formal evening. They go to a relaxing place with a pub-like atmosphere, where they can be 'as they really are'... of course drinking Heineken.

When pre-tested across Europe, the perceived meaning matched what was intended in some, but not all, cultures. In Italy it was understood as it was intended. The young couple chose to be themselves and preferred a genuine, casual evening out where the social interaction was

continues

continued

warm, pure and simple. They were interpreted as modest, but cos-
mopolitan Heineken drinkers. In Greece, however, the pre-test proved
that the ad failed to generate the intended meaning. It was understood
as the young couple not being able to go to a formal event, but instead
having to *settle* for something less. In this context, Heineken was
perceived as being just an ordinary beer for ordinary times. This
meaning clashed with its previous aspirational positioning in Greece.
Instead of strengthening its core identity, Heineken would have down-
graded it with this ad in Greece. In Spain, too, the ad led to Heineken
being perceived as more ordinary than the brand's previous positioning
as an 'upper-class' beer.

In addition to cultural differences, Heineken struggled against
existing brand expectations in repositioning the brand in a more
universal way. It realized that it may perhaps be too soon to standardize
advertising across borders without further examination of the cultural
implications.

The Heineken example illustrates an attempt to move towards the
lower-left quadrant (Q1) on the 'Managing Meaning' matrix (Figure 4.4),
although what Heineken found is that it is still more cost effective to
border on Quadrant 2 (Q2) where the concept is the same but creating
the message that will lead to a common perception is left to local adaptation.

Even with concepts that do, indeed, seem universal, some adaptation
will be required (see Johnson & Johnson, Case 4.2). As will be discussed
below, by considering the positions of various cultures on some of the
cultural dimensions described in Chapter 2, it may be possible to give
more consideration to how to adapt advertisements for different cultural
groups.

Same product concept: local adaptation of message

More typical are examples of strategies designed to increase geographical coverage of products and build local brand strength by globalizing the
brand concept and allowing local adaptation of the message. This tends
to lead to more successful matching of the perceived meaning with the
intended meaning.

For example, since its 1991 reorganization, Unilever Foods has
been keenly focused on re-evaluating its current portfolio of brands and
products with a view to harmonization. Like many consumer products

companies, Unilever is making decisions about which products and brands to keep local, which have a broader scope and which should be dropped. The process has shown that, even if products or brands cannot always be successfully transferred across borders, the concepts and experience behind them can be (Jonquières, 1991). (See Unilever Foods, Case 4.3.)

Box 4.3 The impact of culture on market research

Market research traditionally has explored what people say they do and think or, alternatively, observed what people actually do. In recent years, advertising agencies and ethnologists have been developing approaches to figure out not only *what* consumers do, but *why* they do it. National culture has a direct and obvious impact on any attempt to explore the *why* of consumer behaviour.

Young & Rubicam's Jim Williams has examined existing methodologies to determine their usefulness in cross-cultural market research. Among the various problems, the most fundamental hurdle with all cross-cultural statistical modelling is that identical answers to identical questions in different cultures are not necessarily equivalent. In virtually all statistical analysis procedures there is an assumption that a given value for a given variable should be treated in the same way for all cases in which it is encountered. This, he says, is fine when dealing with objective variables such as height, weight, age, gender and so on, but with subjective variables such as attitudes the same response can mean different things in different cultures.

Difficulties in translation

At the simplest level, some questions cannot even be translated in a meaningful way. For example, on a values questionnaire developed in the USA, the following statements could not easily be translated for use in England:

- 'I am a born-again Christian.'
- 'I like to think I am a bit of a swinger.'

And the English statement:

- 'There are times when it is right to disobey the law.'

in French became:

- '*Il y a des fois où desobéir aux lois est une bonne chose.*'

continues

continued

The French '*une bonne chose*' (a good thing) is far less strict than the intended English meaning of 'right'.

Cultural differences in questionnaire responses

People from different cultures tend to answer in consistently different ways on standardized questionnaires. For example, Germans tend to be overly conservative, marking average or below average even if they have high opinions of a product or think favourably about a particular question. Italians, on the other hand, tend to respond in extremes on standardized questionnaires. So cross-cultural research that relies on mean responses, or even on median responses, may not be giving the information that researchers are looking for.

The same words interpreted in different ways

Understanding anything meaningful from questions such as 'How important is security?', for example, depends on knowing how people in a particular culture regard security. Does security mean your home, your job, a stable family, many friends, or all of these?

Case 4.2   Johnson & Johnson baby products – the language of love

J&J (Johnson & Johnson) has used a 'universal theme' of the love between mother and child to advertise its baby products across cultures. One television ad that travelled particularly well showed a white American mother in bed holding her first, new-born baby. The setting is full of tenderness and love. The music is a soft female voice singing 'The language of love'. Few words are required, the atmosphere speaks for itself.

The language of the song was translated when the ad was screened in a handful of countries, though the same visual was used in the USA, Colombia, New Zealand, Italy, Spain and the Middle East. For South Korea, Malaysia, India and Brazil, however, the white American woman and her baby were replaced by local mothers and babies, in addition to the language change. The film was completely remade, though the film treatment (brand concept) remained the same.

continues

---

continued

In other countries, still further changes were necessary and the ad was reshot again. For example, some of the emotional aspects had to be adapted to the preferences of local cultures. In Australia, where, as in the UK, there is less tolerance for overt expressions of emotion, the emotional aspects were given less prominence and shown only at the end of the ad.

Even with this seemingly universal concept, there were modifications that had to be made to mirror particular cultural realities more appropriately. This ad was certainly successful for J&J in the sense that the consumers' perceived meaning in different markets matched the intended meaning.

Managing the meaning of brands for products and services seems to be the level at which many organizations are globalizing marketing and advertising efforts. Multicultural product teams that are able to agree on product concepts that can be standardized can then rely on local 'insider' companies to execute the messages, so that local consumers will perceive them as intended.

A value-added approach to marketing and advertising across cultures

In attempting to predict how consumers in particular cultures and within certain market segments will perceive the product concepts and the messages, many of the dimensions explored in Chapter 2 can prove useful as a framework (see Figure 4.5). Using an iterative process, an advertiser can consider a product concept and ad in terms of each dimension. This approach potentially gives the advertiser much more information and control over matching intended meaning and perceived meaning. For example, the more the marketers understand about the way a particular culture tends to view status, expressions of emotion, friendship, rules, humour, enjoyment, public life versus private life and so on, the more control they have over creating an ad that will be interpreted in the way in which they want.

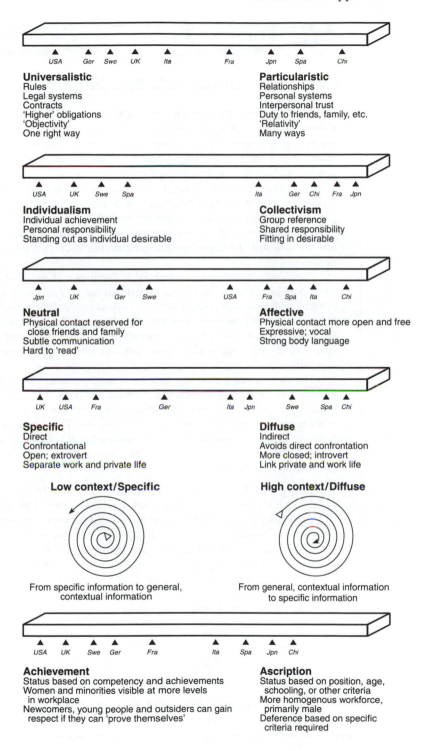

Universalistic
Rules
Legal systems
Contracts
'Higher' obligations
'Objectivity'
One right way

Particularistic
Relationships
Personal systems
Interpersonal trust
Duty to friends, family, etc.
'Relativity'
Many ways

Individualism
Individual achievement
Personal responsibility
Standing out as individual desirable

Collectivism
Group reference
Shared responsibility
Fitting in desirable

Neutral
Physical contact reserved for
  close friends and family
Subtle communication
Hard to 'read'

Affective
Physical contact more open and free
Expressive; vocal
Strong body language

Specific
Direct
Confrontational
Open; extrovert
Separate work and private life

Diffuse
Indirect
Avoids direct confrontation
More closed; introvert
Link private and work life

Low context/Specific

High context/Diffuse

From specific information to general,
contextual information

From general, contextual information
to specific information

Achievement
Status based on competency and achievements
Women and minorities visible at more levels
  in workplace
Newcomers, young people and outsiders can gain
  respect if they can 'prove themselves'

Ascription
Status based on position, age,
  schooling, or other criteria
More homogenous workforce,
  primarily male
Deference based on specific
  criteria required

Figure 4.5   Culture and advertising – considerations of meaning: intended =
perceived?

Case 4.3　Unilever's fish-fingers

Captain Bird's Eye, Captain Findus and Captain Iglo are the different names for Unilever's highly successful fish-fingers brand. Although the product is carefully adapted to local tastes in the various countries where it is sold, and the brand name varies in some countries, the product and advertising concept is the same.

The Foods Executive is responsible for the worldwide strategy of Unilever's food business. It believes that as long as the concept and its presentation are practically identical everywhere, it is not essential to have the same product name and ingredients. Consumers will identify not so much with the Captain's actual name, but with what the Captain personifies.

Fish-fingers are primarily targeted at families with small children. Their positioning has always emphasized that they are a natural seafood product with excellent taste. They are easy to prepare by parents who want only the best for their children. The Captain is the global advertising property and concept to get the message across. The Captain is intended to represent a kind, jolly seaman who is an authority on seafood.

The elements of the ads are important and standardized: a Captain, his ship, the location at sea, children, music and pack shots. While the broad concept is global and standardized, the ads can be modified in accordance with the wishes of the local company. These local adaptations are made to enhance the brand's strength and consistency across cultures. Mr H. Hermsen, marketing manager of Iglo/Ola, the Netherlands, explained:

> 'As long as the advertising message is consistently infused through the different countries and rightly understood, we can say that we have developed an international concept with huge global potential. We are not seeking extreme forms of standardization. It makes no sense if that means that somewhere you will lose part of your market. What matters is that the "Captain" advertising theme is global, understood in the way we intended it to be, and that it supports the global consistency of our brand.'

The analogy between this market concept and the transnational company ideal is close. The search for a powerful global meaning or cultural identity for the company, which can be modified to suit local

Case 4.4   Unisys Corporation – translating customer service into a global message

Unisys, with 1992 sales of $8.4 billion (about half derived outside the USA), specializes in computers, software and computer services for heavy-duty business jobs, such as processing bank cheques and running airline reservations systems. The company was created when Sperry Corporation and Burroughs Corporation merged in 1986. In April 1992, Unisys began using the same creative worldwide, but modifying it for language and cultural differences. According to Robert O'Leary, corporate director of advertising, such a strategy gives Unisys a unified global image and extends a limited ad budget. In his view, implementing a global strategy is easier at Unisys because it sells the same computers, software and services worldwide. In addition, a single international campaign is more likely to register its their target audience – technology managers and senior executives in major companies and government – since they are often frequent international travellers. 'Now they are seeing the same message, the same company, the same look wherever they go,' he explained. 'That really stretches my advertising dollars.'

A recent campaign focused on telling customers to 'customerize', or to improve their customer service, with the help of Unisys. The campaign ran in 47 countries, in 13 languages and 25 dialects. English versions were modified to run in the USA, the UK and Australia, while there were versions in five Spanish and three German dialects. Even with centralized advertising, international managers have some flexibility to change creative both to reflect regional cultural differences and to make sure that regional offices feel they are involved in the process. Such flexibility and adaptation also helps the company avoid potential headquarters' *faux pas*. One ad, for example, shows a map dotted with buildings to illustrate how customers view a company by how close it is to them. Originally, one version of the ad showed a building in the middle of the Amazon while another showed a building on top of an Icelandic glacier. Fortunately, local managers were able to point out the errors and the artwork was retouched.

interests without losing its essential integrity, is the same search for the holy grail.

While this approach has been developed in the light of the aims that companies are trying to achieve and the research available on national cultures, there are cases of advertisers who have used knowledge of cultural differences in sophisticated ways to tailor a campaign. Neville Osrin, former director of international marketing at Steelcase Strafor and now an organizational and cross-cultural consultant for Hewitt Associates in London, provided a very clear example (see Steelcase Strafor, Case 4.5).

Case 4.5   Steelcase Strafor

Steelcase Strafor is a sizeable French office furniture design and retailing organization. In the late 1980s, it was developing a corporate advertising campaign that would run in the top business newspapers and magazines in 10 countries. It was attempting to harmonize the ads as much as possible.

A British advertising agency was used to create the campaign. The advertisement it created featured a photograph of an attractive woman on her way out of the office. The woman looked European, though her nationality was not immediately recognizable. She was smiling and looked very happy. The text for the ad to run in publications in the UK read:

Text
'If you are still smiling when you leave the office, it was designed by Steelcase Strafor.'

Tag line
'Steelcase Strafor. More than a partner, a partnership.'

This ad was very appropriate to the cultural assumptions of the British – especially the separation of work life and private life, the level of emotion in the text (that is formal and direct), and the importance and trust in rules and institutions versus relationships (that is use of 'partnership' as something greater than having a partner) in the tag line.

In France, the same photograph was used but the text was modified in order to have it interpreted with the same meaning. It read:

Text
'For this smile, Strafor designed the office.'

Tag line
'Steelcase Strafor. More than a partner.'

continues

continued

The adaptations to the text made it more effective in the French high-context culture, which is more diffuse and affective. For example, the interpretation of *why* the woman is smiling is left to the imagination of the reader. Does she have a relationship at the office? Is she going to meet someone? The message is more enigmatic, in contrast to the more direct, formal and informative British version.

Furthermore, the tag line was changed, leaving out the phrase 'a partnership'. The reader is not told what it is, if it is more than a partner. That is enough in this high-context culture where relationships are more important than particular universal rules or institutions.

Finally, the Italian version was modified one step further in order to take into consideration the even greater importance of relationships in building trust. The text was the same, but the tag line read:

Tag line
'Steelcase Strafor. More than a partner, a friend.'

Summary

The potential for global brands advertised with global messages seems very limited. There may be a narrow scope at the 'high' end of the market, where consumers of luxury goods have very similar preferences and lifestyles, and at the 'low' end, where there are no pre-existing product expectations, and/or for novel and impulse purchases.

Differences in national culture affect the way in which messages are perceived. In order that effective communication may take place, consumers' *perceived* meaning of a product or service must coincide with the advertiser's *intended* meaning. The most cost-effective way of doing this seems to be to develop a global product and communication concept and to allow for local adaptation of the message.

International marketers can more effectively manage this process, though, by considering the concepts and ads within the framework of how cultures differ on specific cultural dimensions. This provides a way of gaining more understanding of the possible interpretations of the concept and message. The greater knowledge a marketing or advertising executive has about how groups of people view such things as status, humour, information, enjoyment, interpersonal relationships, work life, rules and so on, the more successfully they will be able to manage across cultures.

References

Advertising Age (1993). 15 February, p. 3

Business International (1990). *Marketing Strategies for Global Growth and Competitiveness*. London: Business International

De Jonquières G. (1991). Unilever's food operations. *Financial Times*, 28 October

Gogel R. and Larreche J.C. (1991). Pan-European marketing: combining product strength and geographical coverage. In *Single Market Europe*, (Makridakis, S.G.), pp. 99–118. San Francisco, California: Jossey-Bass

Howard R. (1991). The Designer Organization: Italy's GFT Goes Global. *Harvard Business Review*, September-October

Levitt T. (1983). The globalization of markets. *Harvard Business Review*, May–June

Market-Europe (1993). June

Ohmae K. (1989). Managing in a borderless world. *Harvard Business Review*, May-June

Porter M. (1992). The Strategic Role of International Marketing. In *Global Marketing Management. Cases and Readings*. Boston, Massachusetts: Harvard Business School

5

Managing human resources across cultures

Many aspects of human resource management are affected by differences in national culture. Indeed the very expression of 'human resources' is derived from a cultural framework in which humans are considered to be instruments of production like financial, technical or physical resources. The transaction with human beings is viewed as very specific: the provision of labour in exchange for a specified compensation. This 'objective' exchange of service for compensation separates individuals' personal lives from their work lives in a relationship based on hard economics.

In this Anglo-Saxon world view, a human resource function can be expected to 'manage' these resources, maximizing the value they provide just as the production function is expected to maximize product output and quality. The responsibilities and practices of a human resource function in organizations from these more universalist, Anglo-Saxon cultures will differ from those in many other cultures that do not share this world view. The extent to which human resource management activities are successful across cultures will largely depend on managers' abilities to understand and balance other cultures' values and practices as regards such things as the importance of work, its relationship to the whole person and to the group, how power and status is conferred, the desirability of change, the perceived value of experience versus formal classroom management training and other fundamental differences in how people from different cultures view the world.

This chapter will explore some of the areas where differences in national culture influence human resource management (HRM) across cultures. HRM in this context will refer both to the function of HRM and to the organizational challenge in all cultures of 'managing resourceful humans'.

The context

Two ideas emerging from organizational behaviour literature in recent years help to place the management of human resources across cultures into context. The first comes from the work of Paul Evans and Yves Doz of INSEAD business school in France, and the second from research conducted by Meridith Belbin in the UK.

Evans and Doz have described the managerial challenge in complex international organizations in terms of balancing opposing dualities (Evans and Doz, 1989). They believe that the pace of change and the new complexity of globally operating companies create the need for harmonizing seemingly opposing forces, such as:

Thinking global	Acting local
Decentralization	Centralization
Planned	Opportunistic
Differentiation	Integration
Change	Continuity
Top-down	Bottom-up
Delegation	Control
Competition	Partnership

They urge that such forces should be considered not as binary, either/or decisions, but rather as complementary forces that need to be balanced. The analogy of the human personality is a useful one. Just as any aspect of the personality taken to an extreme is unhealthy and dys-functional, the same is true for organizations. Thus, instead of trying to *maximize* anything (decentralization, teamwork, formality, generalism, and so on), an organization should seek to ensure that it maintains a *minimal threshold* of desirable attributes.

> The normative idea behind a duality is the complementarity of opposites. The growth, prosperity and survival of any social organism, from the human personality studied by Carl Jung to the entire civilizations analysed by historian Arnold Toynbee, depends on striking a dynamic balance between complementary dualities. A social system is in a state of balance only if there is an

equal proportion of the two complementary qualities. However, this balance is dynamic, and not a stationary equilibrium.

The ways in which Evans and Doz advocate balancing dualities in organizations will be discussed later in the context of specific aspects of HRM. This conceptual framework in itself, though, is a useful one in which to consider differences in culture. The whole challenge of managing across cultures, as seen in Chapters 1 and 3, is about balancing seemingly opposing values and practices in such a way as to create advantages from them. Doing so, at the most basic level, requires both recognizing that there is not one right answer that will be consistently or universally applicable and making explicit what the different forces are.

The main idea from the team role research conducted over a 10-year period by the Cambridge University professor Meridith Belbin provides another useful frame in which to consider the impact of culture on various aspects of human resource management (Belbin, 1991). In his original research with high-performing teams, Belbin identified eight 'team roles' that individuals can play when working in teams and that are required for effective team working; these include the Shaper, the Co-ordinator, the Chairman and the Teamworker. The inclusion of people willing or capable of playing each of these roles ensures that the differing skills and qualities required are offered for effective collective performance at different stages of a project, from inception to implementation.

Belbin suggested that each individual has a primary role that he or she tends to feel most comfortable playing, and one to four 'back-up' roles that they are able to play, but which they are less comfortable with. While lower-performing teams were characterized by individuals who collectively could cover only a few of the roles required for effective teamwork, members of high-performing teams had strong diversity of roles and complemented each others' differing strengths. Belbin characterized one consequence of inadequate team role diversity as the 'Apollo syndrome'. He found that groups uniformly made up of highly intelligent people, who individually could have been expected to perform problem-solving well, were, in fact, much less effective than a more balanced, diverse group. The Apollo teams generated internal competition and showed little interest in refining their own effectiveness as a team.

Such observations are particularly relevant to all areas of strategic human resources across cultures and are directly related to the work of Evans and Doz. In addition to recognizing that dualities exist and must be balanced, Belbin's work adds the necessary dimension of considering diversity, or 'dualities', constructively. If Belbin's findings can be generalized to broader organizational functioning in complex, diverse organizations, it is clear that human resource management requirements become less a matter of having the right people at the right place at the right time, and more a matter of integrating selection, reward and appraisal practices within organizational values which will allow a balanced outcome under a range of cultural conditions.

Articulating explicit company values worldwide

Recognizing the increasing importance of new forms of 'glue' or cohesion in global operations, many companies are in the process of developing statements of corporate values worldwide. While some companies opt for the convenient solution of simply translating their statement of values or philosophy and distributing them internationally, the chances that such 'statements' will be interpreted by other cultures as they were intended, or take on any meaningful significance in other cultures, is small.

Instead, companies are finding that cultural differences significantly affect the ability to develop a meaningful statement of company values successfully in at least three important ways:

(1) Cultures assign different meanings to the content and the attainment of stated values.
(2) Employees' actual experiences of a company can differ widely between units or divisions.
(3) If the statement of values does not 'fit' locally, or is different from what local people recognize as reality in their organization, the statement can be more destructive than constructive.

There are three ways in which companies that recognize the impact of cultural differences seem to be taking them into account:

(1) Permitting local interpretations of the statements.
(2) Seeking incorporation of local views as part of the means to create a statement.
(3) Implementing a formal process of multicultural consultation to discuss ways in which the stated values can be applied locally.

The appropriateness of each strategy depends on the degree of commitment to building and reinforcing a common set of values worldwide and the extent to which a set of shared values actually exists.

Lotus, the American computer company, issued its basic values (see Box 5.1) in its operations in different cultures, with the acknowledgement that they might be interpreted differently around the world. It

---

Box 5.1   Lotus – basic values

(1) Commit to excellence
(2) Insist on integrity
(3) Treat people fairly; value diversity
(4) Communicate openly, honestly and directly
(5) Listen with an open mind; learn from everything
(6) Take responsibility; lead by example
(7) Respect, trust and encourage others
(8) Encourage risk-taking and innovation
(9) Establish purpose before action
(10) Work as a team
(11) Have fun!

---

found that, for example, its value 'Commit to excellence' was taken to mean 'getting the best out of yourself' in France, rather than referring to product and service quality. And 'Have fun!', which makes perfect sense in a North American context, was thought to be somewhat intrusive and inappropriate to its Dutch employees. With its statement of values, though, it emphasizes that 'these operating principles are intended to serve as *guidelines* for interaction between all employees. Their purpose is to foster and preserve the spirit of our enterprise and to promote the well-being of all concerned.' Thus the organization allowed for flexibility in the way that employees from different national cultures interpreted the meaning and practice of the basic values.

Other companies, like Motorola, try to gain more consistency in the meaning of their basic values and objectives and to integrate differing interpretations into their implementation. Motorola's statement (see Box 5.2) includes much more detail not only about beliefs, but about what and how goals must be accomplished.

Motorola tries to ensure consistent understanding of these principles across cultures by creating international workshops to discuss them and their implementation in various business sectors and regions. Its consideration of differing interpretations of the stated values and practices of the organization goes a step further than acknowledging that they will happen. It actively discusses interpretations in multicultural teams, and finds culturally appropriate strategies for implementation.

Box 5.2   Motorola: basic values and objectives

Fundamental objective: total customer satisfaction

Key beliefs – how we will always act
- Constant respect for people
- Uncompromising integrity

Key goals – what we must accomplish
- Increased global market share
- Best in class:
  - People
  - Product
  - Marketing
  - Manufacturing
  - Technology
  - Service
- Superior financial results

Key initiatives – how we will do it
- Six sigma quality
- Total cycle time reduction
- Product and manufacturing leadership
- Profit improvement
- Participative management within, and cooperation between organizations

---

Toshiba has taken the process one step further in terms of incorporating different cultural conceptions of the organization into its statement of values. Masaki Mikura at the Tokyo headquarters explained that Toshiba's growth and 1989 restructuring left management wondering 'What is Toshiba?' and 'What does Toshiba believe in?'. While in its domestic market it had a universally recognized name, outside Japan managers were not so certain how, and how consistently, it was perceived by employees, customers, suppliers and local governments. So it believed that it was 'vital for the Toshiba Group to have a cohesive philosophy and identity that could unite companies and employees worldwide and which would provide both the inspiration and the means for further development of its activities'. The company did not want the development of

Box 5.3   Basic commitment of the Toshiba Group

We, the Toshiba Group of companies, based on our total commitment to people and to the future, are determined to help create a higher quality of life for all people, and to do our part to help ensure that progress continues within the world community.

(1) Commitment to people

We endeavour to serve the needs of all people, especially our customers, shareholders and employees, by implementing forward-looking corporate strategies while carrying out responsible and responsive business activities. As good corporate citizens, we actively contribute to further the goals of society.

(2) Commitment to the future

By continually developing innovative technologies centering on the fields of electronics and energy, we strive to create products and services that enhance human life, and which lead to a thriving, healthy society. We constantly seek new approaches that help realize the goals of the world community, including ways to improve the global environment.

Committed to people
Committed to the future
Toshiba

an explicit philosophy to be simply a public relations exercise, or to reflect what the company *would like* the values to be. Rather, it wanted to express the values that were *actually* shared within the organization worldwide.

The beginning of the process was the articulation of what the current president, Mr Aoi, a 35-year Toshiba veteran, believed the spirit of the company was, and should continue to be, in Japanese: *Seii-to-Kigai*, which translates roughly as challenging spirit. Furthermore, he believed there should be an expression of the sincerity that he felt was apparent within the company worldwide.

The public communications group within Toshiba's Tokyo headquarters developed a draft of what they thought the company's basic values were, considering what they might mean in different cultures. They then got the involvement of representative managers at most of their operating companies worldwide to get feedback and input on what those people believed the shared values were. The different interpreta-tions of the text were surprising to the Tokyo group. For example, in Japan, sincerity is more to do with your real feelings towards others, be it customers, co-workers and so on. It is very much directed outwards and concerns sincere relationships with others. They discovered that in the USA and parts of Europe, though, managers interpreted sincerity to be more about being frank and natural yourself. The term, they felt, reflected more of an inner truthfulness than something to do primarily with relationships, though they agreed with the intended meaning of the term.

After two more drafts and considering the input and interpretations of different national managers, the Basic Commitment of the Toshiba Group was developed (see Box 5.3).

From several interviews with managers in different countries, this does seem actually to reflect Toshiba's management system, encompass the views and perspectives of many of its operating companies and have meaning for people within the organization in different cultures.

'Every act of creation is an act of destruction'[†]

If an organization is attempting to gain the strategic capabilities of a 'transnational', such as building flexibility and learning into the organi-zation worldwide and creating competitive advantages from diversity, all aspects of HRM must reflect these qualities. Yet the process of articulat-ing specific values that are desirable to the organization means implicitly stating the values that are undesirable. In the context of Evans and Doz's work, the more complex and diverse an organism, the greater the neces-sity of balancing opposing forces rather than making either/or choices. If, for example, a stated company value is 'entrepreneurship', and this is a quality against which people are selected, rewarded and promoted, it can lead to a company that is very capable of taking new initiatives but very poor at following through, behaving cohesively or working together towards a global strategy. While a single, specified set of culture-specific values may be appropriate for a company operating in a relatively stable industry in a single domestic market, it does not seem appropriate to a complex, globally operating organization.

The values that do seem appropriate to extend across cultures are less about culture-specific qualities and more about ways of interacting with people who are different from yourself. In fact, several experts in the field of managing cultural differences seem to think that this is what the

[†]Picasso

likely corporate culture of a global organization will be about. Vincent O'Neill, deputy director of Management Language and Intercultural Training at Siemens, thinks that human resource issues are like the other dilemmas in a global company. In this context, 'There is a field of tensions where you are holding things together that are basically operating in different directions. In German we call it a *Spannungsfeld* .' With regard to trying to articulate explicit company values worldwide, Mr O'Neill says:

'If you reduce the tenets of a corporate culture to the lowest common denominator, then you have a vague philosophical statement which doesn't distinguish you from any other major corporation. They all say the same thing: "our success depends on our people", "customer satisfaction is our first priority", and so on. So the question is, doesn't it make more sense to say "small is, in fact, beautiful" and that small units have their own corporate culture? That is the way things are going. And what we then have to do is to create a bracket that will hold the tensions together. And whether you can do that internationally with a corporate culture that comes from headquarters is a big question in my mind. If you take the Ikea approach [see Chapter 3], for example, you run the risk of losing the value of diversity. It is very difficult, I think, to find brackets which will satisfy everyone. I think the way things will develop in the future is that you say that we have a *developing* corporate culture which has to do with the way people treat each other. That means that your corporate culture is flexible, but it is still a bracket.

'Maintaining this bracket involves certain kinds of instruments in the widest sense of the word. Say, for instance, as part of your human resource policy and development you have a policy of staff dialogue. We have in our situation staff dialogue which should be performed annually with each member of your staff. It is on average 2–3 hours. It is a discussion on equal terms of the results, of what affected the results – good or bad, of setting goals for the future, and dealing with the areas of motivation, criticism, analysis of developments of the past year and projecting into the future. If you take that seriously then it is very, very effective. But it is complex and complicated by diversity. In my own team I have German, Irish, Welsh, French, Spanish and South American nationalities represented. That dialogue is very important, but it is different from one culture to another. In other words, their views of motivation, leadership, decision-making and so on are different from each other and different from mine. And the majority of us are non-German, but operating in a German culture. So there are levels of complexity which you have to deal with. And that is similar to a corporate culture. That is why I say the flexible brackets are so important and they can only be based on how we deal with one another. And if that is working, then it will work for the customer as well.'

Selection

Approaches to selection vary significantly across cultures. There are differences not only in the priorities that are given to technical or interpersonal capabilities, but also in the ways that candidates are tested and interviewed for the desired qualities.

In Anglo-Saxon cultures, what is generally tested is how much the individual can contribute to the tasks of the organization. In these cultures, assessment centres, intelligence tests and measurements of competencies are the norm. In Germanic cultures, the emphasis is more on the quality of education in a particular function. The recruitment process in Latin and Far Eastern cultures is very often characterized by ascertaining how well the person 'fits in' with the larger group. This is determined in part by the elitism of higher educational institutions, such as the *grandes écoles* in France or the University of Tokyo in Japan, and in part by their interpersonal style and ability to network internally. If there are tests in Latin cultures, they will tend to be more about personality, communication and social skills than about the Anglo-Saxon notion of 'intelligence'.

Though there are few statistical comparisons of selection practices used across cultures, one recent study provides a useful example of the impact of culture. A survey conducted by Shackleton and Newell compared selection methods between France and the UK. They found that there was a striking contrast in the number of interviews used in the selection process, with France resorting to more than one interview much more frequently. They also found that in the UK there is a much greater tendency to use panel interviews than in France, where one-to-one interviews are the norm. In addition, while almost 74% of companies in the UK use references, only 11.3% of the companies surveyed in France used them. Furthermore, French companies rely much more on personality tests and handwriting analysis than do British ones (Shackleton and Newell, 1991).

The differences between cultures in terms of the qualities considered most important and the methodologies used to assess them can be better understood in the light of their relative positions on the cultural dimen-

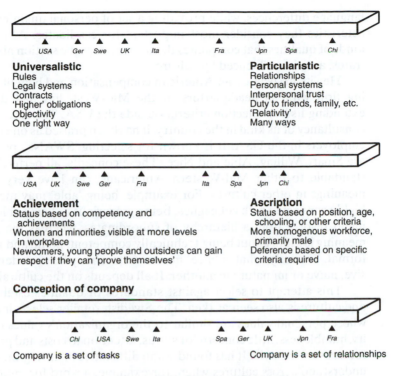

Universalistic
Rules
Legal systems
Contracts
'Higher' obligations
Objectivity
One right way

Particularistic
Relationships
Personal systems
Interpersonal trust
Duty to friends, family, etc.
'Relativity'
Many ways

Achievement
Status based on competency and
    achievements
Women and minorities visible at more levels
    in workplace
Newcomers, young people and outsiders can gain
    respect if they can 'prove themselves'

Ascription
Status based on position, age,
    schooling, or other criteria
More homogenous workforce,
    primarily male
Deference based on specific
    criteria required

Conception of company

Company is a set of tasks

Company is a set of relationships

Figure 5.1   Culture and selection.

sions of universalism/particularism, achievement/ascription and the differences in how people from different cultures conceive of the organization (see Figure 5.1).

As the survey of French and British selection methods illustrates, more universalist and achievement-oriented cultures tend to rely more on 'objective' measurable criteria about individuals' intellectual or technical capabilities in order to assess their 'fit' to a set of tasks. More particularist cultures, on the other hand, rely more on information about an individual's personality and potential for trust in order to assess a more relationship-oriented notion of 'fit'. For example, the higher frequency of interviews used in France makes sense if French assumptions are more about individuals' ability to function successfully within a web of relationships and hierarchies, as opposed to simply having the skills required by the job. Furthermore, the use of panel interviews and intelligence tests in the UK assumes that the qualities being assessed are 'objective', measurable qualities that are either there or not. The rapport between the interviewee and interviewers is less of a consideration.

Many organizations operating across cultures have tended to decentralize selection in order to allow for local differences in testing and for language differences, while providing a set of personal qualities or characteristics they consider most important for candidates. Although the kinds of qualities that companies deem critical, as the section above illustrates, are also influenced by culture.

Hewitt Associates, an American compensation and benefits consulting firm with its headquarters in the Mid-West, has had difficulties extending its key selection criteria outside the USA. The second largest consultancy of its kind in the country, it has been praised as one of the top employers in the USA. It is known for selecting 'SWANs': people who are Smart, Willing, Able and Nice. These concepts, all perfectly understandable to other Mid-Western Americans, can have very different meanings in other cultures. For example, being 'able' may mean being highly connected with colleagues, being gregarious or being able to command respect from a hierarchy of subordinates, whereas the intended meaning is more about being technically competent, polite and relatively formal. Similarly, what is 'nice' in one culture may be considered intrusive, naïve or immature in another. It all depends on the cultural context.

This attempt to select against standards or qualities established in one culture is also seen at Ikea. The Swedish retailer selects individuals whose personal values are similar to the organization's values of frugality, humbleness, little concern for status, attention to costs and preference for a casual lifestyle. It has found some difficulties in having these values understood across cultures when, for example, a word for 'humbleness' does not even exist in French.

Other companies, like Shell, Toyota and L'Oréal, have identified very *specific* qualities that they consider strategically important and that support their business requirements. For example, the criteria that Shell has identified as most important in supporting its strategy include mobility and language capability. These are more easily understood across cultures because people are either willing to relocate or not, and are able to speak, or willing to learn, other languages, or not. There is less room for cultural misunderstandings with such qualities.

When the qualities identified for selection are very culture- and value-specific, they do not provide for the complexity and diversity that exist within globally operating organizations. The interpretations and importance that people from different cultures give to them can be very different from those intended. Identifying those more concrete, specific criteria that agree with the strategic requirements of the organization may leave less room for differing interpretations. However, identifying the managerial qualities that support the values of the organization does not lend itself to such one-dimensional descriptions.

As in the previous section, it seems more appropriate to base any global selection criteria on the complex managerial requirements of 'balance'. This will be explored in detail in the section on performance appraisal below.

Career development

Culture influences the ways in which organizations understand and practice career development, as well as the career goals and expectations of individuals from different cultures. This section will explore different models of career development typical of organizations in particular cultures, and describe some of the cultural preferences behind the approaches. A review of the impact of culture on individual managers' conception of career is also given.

Organizational models of career development

Paul Evans, Elizabeth Lank and Alison Farquar have identified and described four different organizational approaches based on cultural differences: Anglo-Dutch, Germanic, Japanese and Latin (Evans *et al*, 1989).

The Anglo-Dutch approach (Figure 5.2) is dominated by the idea of developing managers. Selection for development is usually done in the

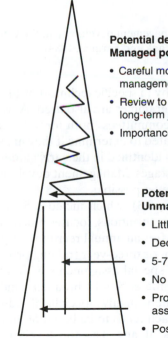

Potential development:
Managed potential development

• Careful monitoring of high potentials by management review committees

• Review to match up performance and potential with short- and long-term job and development requirements

• Importance of management development staff

Potential identification:
Unmanaged functional trial

• Little elite recruitment

• Decentralized recruitment for technical or functional jobs

• 5-7 years' trial

• No corporate monitoring

• Problem of internal potential identification via assessments, assessment centres, indicators

• Possible complementary recruitment of high potentials

Figure 5.2   Managed development approach to management development: the Anglo-Dutch model. (*Source*: Evans, Lank and Farquar, 1989)

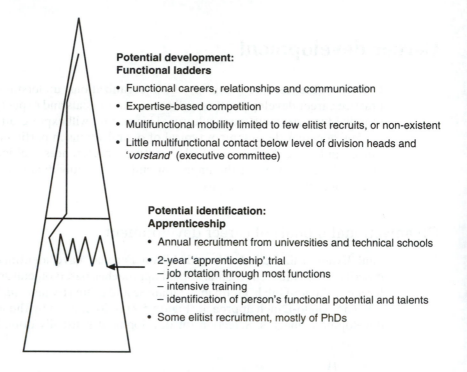

Potential development:
Functional ladders

- Functional careers, relationships and communication
- Expertise-based competition
- Multifunctional mobility limited to few elitist recruits, or non-existent
- Little multifunctional contact below level of division heads and '*vorstand*' (executive committee)

Potential identification:
Apprenticeship

- Annual recruitment from universities and technical schools
- 2-year 'apprenticeship' trial
  – job rotation through most functions
  – intensive training
  – identification of person's functional potential and talents
- Some elitist recruitment, mostly of PhDs

Figure 5.3   Functional approach to management development: the Germanic model. (*Source*: Evans, Lank and Farquar, 1989)

first five to seven years in the company in specific technical or functional jobs. High-potential recruitment programmes are also used. Assessment centres and/or management review committees (both formal and informal) are where individuals are evaluated to determine if they are serving the goals of the company. Potential is identified in the early career stages and monitored carefully in the later stages. Management development is taken seriously and formalized wherever possible.

The Germanic approach (Figure 5.3), which includes Switzerland and some Dutch and Scandinavian organizations, focuses much more on preparation for functional careers. After an annual recruitment process, candidates typically go through a two- or three-year training programme that combines in-company jobs and special assignments with intensive training. This development programme serves to broaden candidates' knowledge after emerging from their highly specialized education. Competition in this Germanic approach tends to be based on functional expertise, with very few generalists, if any. The top levels of many German companies will usually carry the title Doctor or Professor.

The Japanese model that emerged in large companies after the Second World War is highly competitive (Figure 5.4). It is based on

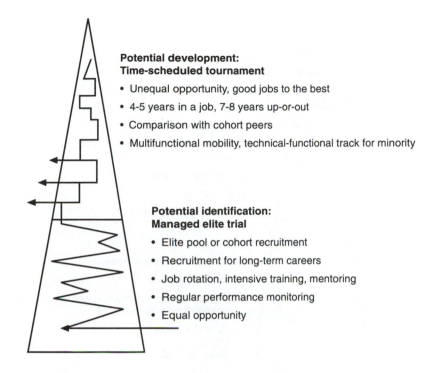

Potential development:
Time-scheduled tournament

• Unequal opportunity, good jobs to the best

• 4-5 years in a job, 7-8 years up-or-out

• Comparison with cohort peers

• Multifunctional mobility, technical-functional track for minority

Potential identification:
Managed elite trial

• Elite pool or cohort recruitment

• Recruitment for long-term careers

• Job rotation, intensive training, mentoring

• Regular performance monitoring

• Equal opportunity

Figure 5.4   Elite cohort approach to management development: the Japanese
model. (*Source*: Evans, Lank and Farquar, 1989)

recruitment of an elite cohort from top universities. The functions they
are initially placed in may or may not have anything to do with their formal course of study. At Toyota and Nissan all newcomers must spend a
period of a few months working on the shop floor. For the first four or
five years there is no further screening; management development is
identified by entry.

Performance is monitored, usually several times annually, by powerful personnel departments. There is a high degree of rotation between
functions. The cohorts recruited in a particular year are promoted
together. Promotions are expected every four to five years or else the
candidate is generally out of the running for more senior positions.

Within the largest Latin international companies, entry is also very
elitist (Figure 5.5). As in the Japanese model, a great deal of status is conferred by the university attended. In France, for example, a study showed
that a graduate of the *grande école* had a 90% chance of becoming a company president. In this model, the organization is a real political system,
where career development is largely based on visible achievements,
mentors and coalitions. After obtaining a degree from one of the right

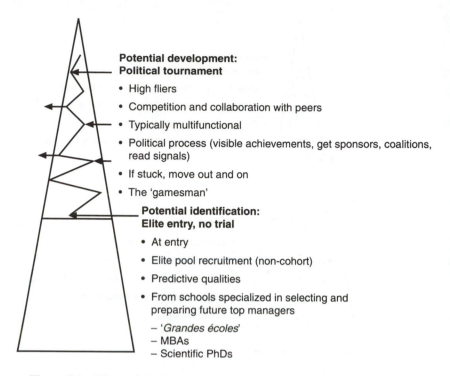

Potential development:
Political tournament

- High fliers
- Competition and collaboration with peers
- Typically multifunctional
- Political process (visible achievements, get sponsors, coalitions, read signals)
- If stuck, move out and on
- The 'gamesman'

Potential identification:
Elite entry, no trial

- At entry
- Elite pool recruitment (non-cohort)
- Predictive qualities
- From schools specialized in selecting and preparing future top managers
  - 'Grandes écoles'
  - MBAs
  - Scientific PhDs

Figure 5.5 Elite political approach to management development: the Latin model. (*Source*: Evans, Lank and Farquar, 1989)

institutions, career development is about making connections and impressing the right people.

Many of the differences identified in approaches to career development can be better understood in terms of the cultural dimensions of ascription/achievement, universalism/particularism, specific/diffuse relationships and individualism/collectivism (see Chapter 2 for full descriptions). For example, the more individualist, achievement-oriented and universalist Anglo-Dutch model relies more on assessment centres and review committees to identify potential and to determine the extent to which the individual is serving the *goals* of the organization. This assumes that:

(1) Potential is 'objective' and measurable.
(2) People must 'prove' themselves in the tasks they were hired to perform.
(3) Almost anyone (relatively speaking), regardless of age, family background or connections, can 'make it' if they can achieve in their specific capacity.

In the more particularistic, ascriptive and diffuse Japanese and Latin models, the organization is much less of a functional system and more of a 'human' system. Entry is determined more by elite institutions and relationships than the relatively more functional, achievement-oriented criteria of the other two models.

Culture also plays a role in determining the career expectations and goals of managers.

How individuals from different cultures perceive the career

Recent research by André Laurent and Brooke Derr helps to shed some light on the impact of culture on individuals' conceptions of career, in particular the way they would answer the question: 'What do I want from work, given my perceptions of who I am and what is possible?' Their research has shown that national culture has a significant effect on what individuals from particular cultures are socialized to expect and want from their career (Laurent and Derr, 1989).

To explore the role of national culture in career, Laurent approached a large US-based multinational because of its high professional reputation in human resource management. This company had for years implemented a standardized worldwide system for the multiple assessment of managerial potential and performance. The research objective was to assess whether this common administrative system would standardize managers' perceptions of career success criteria across various national affiliated companies. During interviews with a representative sample of 100 upper-middle managers throughout the organization, Laurent asked such questions as: 'In your view, what does it take to be successful at XY?' National samples were then conducted in five affiliated companies in France, West Germany, the Netherlands, the UK and the USA. The following 10 items were chosen most frequently by the group of 262 respondents:

 (1) Ambition and drive (82%)
 (2) Leadership ability (77%)
 (3) Skills in interpersonal relations and communication (75%)
 (4) Being labelled as having high potential (72%)
 (5) Managerial skills (69%)
 (6) Achieving results (69%)
 (7) Self-confidence (65%)
 (8) Creative mind (60%)
 (9) Ability to handle interfaces between groups (58%)
(10) Hard work (58%)

There were important differences between the five national groups in spite of the convergence that could be expected from a similar worldwide career system. The most significant cross-cultural variations were the following:

- While only 57% of Dutch managers selected skills in interpersonal relations and communication as a most important determinant of career success, 89% of British managers did.
- Being labelled as having high potential was perceived as most important by 54% of Germans compared with 81% of the French.
- Achieving results had a high American score of 88% and a low French score of 52%. Similarly, 81% of Americans selected self-confidence while only 42% of the French did so.
- A creative mind was perceived as the top success criterion by Germans (77%) while it was seen as much less relevant by the French.

The results also revealed important differences in the degree of consensus (or understanding) concerning the success criteria *within* each national affiliate. While six criteria were selected as most important for career success by more than 80% of American managers, the corresponding figures were three criteria for the British, one for the Dutch and the French and none for the Germans. Laurent summarized this as that the degree of perceptual clarity, fit and comfort with the overall career success culture of the firm was much higher for American managers, who were, of course, culturally closer to the system designers. Furthermore, he gave the following overview of his findings concerning the German, British and French managers:

> 'German managers, more than others, believe that creativity is essential for career success. In their mind, the successful manager is the one who has the right individual characteristics. Their outlook is rational: they view the organization as a coordinated network of individuals who make appropriate decisions based on their professional competence and knowledge.
>
> 'British managers hold a more interpersonal and subjective view of the organizational world. According to them, the ability to create the right image and to get noticed for what they do is essential for career success. They view the organization primarily as a network of relationships between individuals who get things done by influencing each other through communicating and negotiating.
>
> 'French managers look at the organization as an authority network where the power to organize and control the actors stems from their positioning in the hierarchy. They focus on the organization as a pyramid of differentiated levels of power to be acquired or dealt with. French managers perceive the ability to manage power relationships effectively and to 'work the system' as particularly critical to their success.'

Laurent's summary matches the implicit models of organization held in different national cultures as discussed in Chapter 3. It is important for international managers to understand these differences. As human resource managers balance the centralization/decentralization tension in career development, these cultural implications can prove useful in striking the right balance. On the one hand, managers must recognize that centralizing career development worldwide can lead to 'high-potential' managers misunderstanding or being frustrated by the system because of their differing career expectations and goals, or because the system employed does not prepare managers with the set of experiences *they* consider valuable or marketable outside the firm. There may also be difficulties gaining cooperation from local HR personnel or from operational people responsible for identifying candidates for career development if they do not agree with the approach. Decentralization, on the other hand, can pose great difficulties in gaining any coherence in a global career development system.

Performance appraisal

The process of performance appraisal attempts to influence and motivate consistent behaviour. For organizations operating across cultures, identifying qualities against which to appraise, select, reward and promote people internationally is so complex that it often defeats the appraisal system time and again. It is usually an attempt to induce managers to communicate and reward those aspects of performance that the organization wants to universally encourage.

As revealed in the study by Laurent and Derr described in the last section, individuals from different cultures give different meanings and different levels of importance to managerial qualities. Applying the concept of dualities to performance appraisal, this implies that defining appraisal criteria is not simply a matter of identifying appraisal qualities that can be used universally or, alternatively, allowing managers in each culture to develop their own qualities to appraise against. Rather, it is recognizing that:

(1)   There are differences in the qualities that are important and valued in different cultures.
(2)   For each quality that can be identified there is an equally attractive opposite.

In Japan, for example, there is more of an emphasis on encouraging teamwork, while in many Western cultures there is more emphasis on encouraging the individual as an entrepreneur. An Eastern approach might call for holism and generalization, while a Western approach calls more for analysis and specialization. Latins might emphasize intuition and flexibility, and the Germanic cultures might prefer self-control and structure. No approach is inherently superior; all have their merits. Just as some Japanese companies have been introducing Western-style incentives to balance their approach, some Western companies are trying to find ways to balance theirs.

BP and Shell are both major oil companies, technically showing many things in common. However, their cultures have evolved over many years to create quite distinctive differences in their approaches to HRM and to culture management.

When Mr Horton, an Englishman, arrived as CEO fresh from success in the USA, where he grew a justified reputation as a tough cost-cutter, the man who turned around the ailing Sohio, he quickly made his mark on headquarters. He surveyed the company and decided that the culture had to change. It was too bureaucratic, too centralized, too slow moving, too far from customer needs. With help, he created a model of a new, global culture which BP was going to have as part of Project 1990. Four clusters of competencies were identified, creating the mnemonic OPEN:

(1)   Open thinking
(2)   Personal impact
(3)   Empowering
(4)   Networking

Each of these were, in Anglo-Saxon terms, unexceptional except that the supporting competencies were occasionally contradictory. For example, 'promotes diversity' and 'breaks down cultural barriers' were both part of open thinking. The main issue came where OPENness was mandated across such diverse national cultures as Belgium, France, the Netherlands, Germany, Spain, the USA, Singapore and Japan. Take one example, 'empowering' – giving away authority – To a Dutchman, whose heroes are the quiet men, empowering is a perfectly normal practice; to a Frenchman it would be abandonment.

Shell, born of a dual culture generations ago and highly aware of and almost obsessed by its internationalism, had adopted the more integrative, balanced approach that is required if firms are to truly value diversity and use it effectively. Shell has experimented with introducing a set of balancing traits in its performance appraisal. For example, next to power of analysis (the ability to break down a problem and look at its components) it placed power of synthesis (the ability to see connections and relationships, and to draw broad conclusions). Both of these are important qualities for successful managers. Some of the other 'constructive tensions' that Evans and Doz consider are:

Sense of reality	Imagination
Rational thinking	Intuitive thinking
Control	Entrepreneurship
Vision	Reality
Action	Reflection
Flexibility	Focus

Performance appraisal, like selection and career development, can be more effective across cultures if cultural values, expectations and advantages can be considered and included in determining the balance of qualities most important to the organization.

The role of HRM professionals in a multicultural world

It could be expected that with this demand for ever greater sophistication in managing people across cultures the importance of the HRM professional would be growing. That is not so. The evidence across the world is that if anything their status is declining.

Tom Lester has researched human resources management in Europe, and made a preliminary report in *International Management* (Lester, 1994). He pointed out that:

'According to a survey of 11 countries conducted by a group of nine European business schools and the accounting and consultancy firm Price Waterhouse, the human resources head is represented on the main board of 87% of large Swedish companies, but only 19% of German companies and 18% of Italian companies. In no more than half the enterprises in any country are human resources involved from the outset in the formulation of corporate strategy.'

One real problem for the HRM professionals is that their roots are in the defence of the employee rather than in the pursuit of strategy. Changing the name from IR, or Personnel, did not take away responsibility for supporting the compliance with social legislation such as in Germany, France and Italy where the personnel managers have legal responsibilities to represent employees. Strategic issues almost become the antithesis to these roles.

Where the HR manager will make the difference, and here perhaps is the real justification of the change in title, is growing the managerial and technical competencies required to survive in this changing world. Tom Lester again:

'As companies seek to be more entrepreneurial and customer-oriented, and to make the best use of management potential whether it arises in Seville or Singapore, so the development of able young managers becomes crucial. It is a traditional human resources function given urgent strategic importance by the competitive pressure of contemporary business.

'At Bertelsmann, the privately owned German publishing and entertainment group, the corporate motto coined by founder Reinhard Mohn is "every manager an entrepreneur".

'"The company's goal is to provide a work environment where people can grow", says Klaus Papenfuss, human resources director of the books division, which embraces Bantam and Doubleday in the USA. His role is to recruit "intelligent and hard young high flyers" from the best international business schools, and to see that they are given early responsibility in the 30 small publishing houses that make up the division. Management development courses teach them how to buy companies in different countries, to speak the languages and to understand cultural differences. In newly acquired companies, Papenfuss and his team are required to assess and help assimilate the best of the acquired management.'

Summary

Differences in national culture affect the very notion of human resource management, as well as particular aspects of the function. Indeed, the very idea of a separate functional area being able to 'manage' human beings is an Anglo-Saxon cultural preference; many other cultures would not share this understanding of human resources. Within the management aspects generally under the responsibility of a human resource function, the impact of culture is also very apparent.

Culture influences how companies from different cultures select individuals, the methodologies they use and the technical or personal qualities that are considered important. While Anglo-Saxon cultures tend to focus more on the ability of an individual to perform a particular set of tasks and employ such practices as assessment centres, intelligence tests and panel interviews, more particularist and ascriptive cultures tend to rely more on how well the individual fits into the larger group and to employ personality or social skills tests or limit selection to particular educational institutions.

The qualities that are considered important to success in different cultures also vary, and, for international organizations trying to define specific criteria for selection, career development and performance appraisal, it is important to take the differences into consideration. The framework of Evans and Doz provides a useful way of considering diversity in complex, rapidly changing organizations. The challenge for managers in such environments becomes balancing many seemingly 'opposing' forces, rather than making binary either/or choices. And, as Meridith Belbin's work reminds us, it is precisely in balancing diverse qualities and capabilities that the most effective teamworking and management occur. Valuing, selecting and promoting 'PLUs' (People Like Us) makes for greater organizational comfort but de-optimizes organizational performance, flexibility and potential for learning.

References

Belbin R.M. (1991). *Management Teams: Why They Succeed or Fail*. London: Heinemann

Evans P. and Doz Y. (1989). The dualistic organization. In *Human Resource Management in International Firms: Change, Globalization, Innovation* (Evans P., Doz Y. and Laurent A., eds.). pp. 219–242. London: Macmillan

Evans P., Lank E. and Farquar A. (1989). Managing human resources in the international firm: lessons from practice. In *Human Resource Management in International Firms: Change, Globalization, Innovation* (Evans P., Doz Y. and Laurent A., eds.). London: Macmillan

Laurent A. and Derr C. B. (1989). The internal and external career: a theoretical and cross-cultural perspective. In *Handbook of Career Theory* (Arthur M., Hall D. and Lawrence B., eds.). Cambridge: Cambridge University Press

Lester T. (1994). Close the Personnel Department?, *International Management*, April

Shackleton V.V. and Newell S. (1991). Management selection: a comparative survey of methods used in top British and French companies. *Journal of Occupational Psychology*, **64**, 23–36

6

Managing alliances across cultures

Strategic rationale for alliances

Strategic alliances have increasingly become a critical component of global strategy. Whether they provide market access, product or technological expertise, greater economies of scale, and risk sharing or simply spread development or marketing costs, alliances can offer important advantages in a number of ways. They allow a company to capture new skills, new products and new markets, and to do it very quickly. But they also bring their own characteristic management problems in addition to the normal management challenges of running a business. One of the central problems in alliances is learning. Alliances express the need to learn. Most companies use them to draw resources *into* the company. The problems of managing alliances are the problems of capturing these resources – and this requires the ability to learn across cultures (Business International, 1990).

The high probability of failure in alliances is now common knowledge. Estimates of the success rate of cross-border alliances and acquisitions range from only about one-third to one-half. Some recent studies (Buchanan and Berman, 1992) of strategic alliances have turned up interesting data on the common causes of failure and recommendations for success (see Figure 6.1 and Box 6.2). Conspicuously absent from these studies and from much of the other cross-border alliance research is the role of cultural differences in the different phases of managing alliances across cultures.

Box 6.1   East European managers accuse Westerners of aggressiveness

Many managers in Hungary, Poland and the Czech Republic accuse Westerners imported through alliances and joint ventures to teach them how to be capitalists of being aggressive and insensitive to local culture, according to a study published by GKR/Neumann, a London-based executive search company (*Financial Times*, 1992). In a study of 300 local and Western managers working in the three countries, it appears that all sides agree that while joint ventures and alliances have created beneficial opportunities, 'culture gaps' between executives are seriously delaying cross-cultural learning and the transfer of expertise. While local managers have a theoretical grasp of, for example, pricing policy, the study reports, practical implementation is slow and beset by temporary setbacks. The two groups blame each other for the stumbling progress. In Hungary, almost 50% of local managers objected to Western managers, while in the Czech Republic and Poland, about 75% said Westerners were merely tolerated. Western managers surveyed complained about such problems as keeping anything secret in Hungary, of the importance and difficulties of becoming an 'insider' in Poland, and of the constant need to give and ask for feedback with Czech managers.

Bain & Company summarized its findings of what commonly causes alliances to fail:

- Inadequate up-front planning on such issues as structure, ownership, control and exit options.
- Mismanaged expectations of the alliance partners, of the alliance itself and of the outside world.
- Lack of balance between the relative contributions to, and dependence on, the outcome of the alliance.

Consistently, studies of acquisitions, mergers and alliances have emphasized the need for extensive preparation, a relationship of trust between negotiators and a long period of post-alliance consolidation. It is a difficult business, at its most successful when the two parties are alike, and showing progressively less chance as differences of all kinds widen.

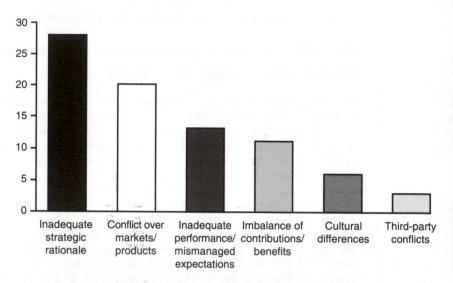

Figure 6.1 Pitfalls of strategic alliances: frequency and common causes of failure. (*Source*: Buchanan and Berman, 1992)

Box 6.2 Recommendations for successful cross-border alliances

In a recent study of cross-border alliances, the McKinsey & Company consulting firm examined partnerships of 150 top companies ranked by market value (Bleeke and Ernst, 1991). Included were 50 each from the USA, Europe and Japan. The recommendations given in the report were based on the experience of the successful partnerships.

- Alliances between strong and weak companies rarely work. They do not provide the missing skills needed for growth, and they lead to mediocre performance.
- Cross-border alliances and acquisitions have a higher success rate (51% and 57% respectively) than home-country acquisitions (25%), primarily because cross-border alliances tend to be in the core business whereas domestic alliances are more likely to be in related, but non-core businesses.
- Mergers and acquisitions have better success when there is moderate or high geographical overlap, but alliances do better if there is minimal geographical overlap.
- Alliances with equal strength and equal ownership tend to be more successful. Where both partners are strong, there is greater success in an alliance. With equal ownership, better decisions for the venture are made rather than decisions benefiting just one parent.

continues

continued

- Flexibility is a hallmark of successful alliances. Flexibility allows joint ventures to overcome problems, adapt to changes over time and resolve conflicts.
- A partnership is most likely to succeed when there is a strong, independent management team and a strong board with operational decision-making responsibility.

The role of culture in alliances across cultures

Each of the common causes of failure in alliances illustrated by Bain & Company, as well as the McKinsey recommendations, is implicitly affected bycultural differences. In the Bain study, for example, inadequate strategic rationale, conflict over markets/products, mismanaged expectations, imbalance of contributions and third-party conflicts are all about interactions between managers from each side of the alliance. The ability to understand differing strategic rationales, to come to agreement on markets and products, and to manage potentially differing expectations and contributions depends on the ability to understand and appreciate differing cultural assumptions. As seen in the previous chapters, the meanings of markets, products and organizations differ across cultures, as do expectations about managing, motivating, security, risk, growth strategies, and so on. Although 'cultural differences' was isolated as a separate category of pitfall in the Bain findings, it is actually an underlying reason for all of the pitfalls identified.

Similarly, in many of the recommendations given in the McKinsey study, the role of culture is implicit. While it is obviously necessary to understand the strategic prerequisites for successful cross-cultural alliances, such as minimal geographical overlap and linkages between equally strong companies in core business areas, the cultural implications of these findings have been largely ignored. Consider the key findings.

Cross-border alliances should:

- Be between strong companies.
- Be in core business areas.
- Have minimal geographic overlap.
- Be between partners of equal strength.
- Be flexible, able to resolve conflicts.
- Have strong, independent management.

Each of these recommendations increases both the likelihood of success *and* the probability of conflict. In an acquisition of a weaker company by a stronger, obviously you would expect the acquirer to impose its own practices on the acquired company because it has been more successful and can share its knowledge. With two equally strong companies in an alliance starting from differing cultural preferences, the direction of influence is not as clear. Furthermore, if the alliance is in each partner's core business, the importance placed on the venture's success and the ensuing pressure and involvement from each partner are likely to be significant. Additionally, a firm's alliance partner in one business is likely to be a competitor in another, adding an element of secrecy and distrust to the already complicated equation. In order to manage successfully the complexity of a cross-cultural alliance that meets these requisites, managers must be able to decipher and appreciate different cultural assumptions and practices in at least the following phases of managing a cross-cultural alliance:

- Understanding the differing goals and expectations of a potential partner.
- The negotiation process: who attends, how it proceeds, the purpose of and reliance on meetings and legal agreements versus relationships and trust.
- The integration process: deciding which company supplies which managers, deciding on what the culture of the alliance should be, negotiating policies and procedures, merging company cultures.
- The management process: reaching decisions without endless delays and battles.

In the joint venture between Toshiba (Japanese) and Motorola (American), the cultural assumptions behind each of these phases were considered and managed just as effectively as the strategic and financial aspects of the alliance.

Case 6.1   Joint venture between Motorola and Toshiba

The Toshiba–Motorola alliance has been highlighted as an example of two partners striking the right balance: both were industry giants and brought particular, complementary expertise to the partnership. All aspects of this joint venture, formed in Japan on 11 May, 1987, meet the 'success' guidelines found in the McKinsey study (see above).

continues

continued

'This was a different kind of joint venture which was unusual in the industry,' Mr Shima, the first president of the joint venture, now back at Toshiba, explained.

'Both companies were transferring their excellent, number one technology to the joint venture. We both came to the alliance to enhance technology, to make an excellent product and to transfer aspects of what we learned to the parent companies.

'If we could take Toshiba's excellence in memory and process technology and Motorola's excellence in microprocessor technology and make these into one, both companies would be better off.'

The relationship between the parent companies was further linked by arrangements whereby Motorola could gain assistance from Toshiba in penetrating the semiconductor market in Japan. At the time Japan had a 40% share of the world consumption of semiconductors.

The impact of culture

Of the differences in culture that arose throughout the process, the two that were particularly noticeable to Mr Shima were:

- Decisions in the USA were often more top-down than in Japan.
- There were different notions of loyalty between employees and the company.

From the perspective of the former vice-president of Nippon Motorola, Richard Timmins (an American), the aspects of culture that were most apparent were how meetings were conducted, the level of detail that each side expected in negotiations, and some differences in human resource practices.

Different ways of conducting meetings and negotiations

Mr Timmins explained:

'How we conducted meetings was different. They [Japanese managers] tend to be very detailed in meetings whereas we [American managers] are used to discussing things in general terms, agreeing to the important concepts, and then letting the lawyers and more technical people put the details in writing. It seemed that it was opposite, though, with there being very detailed meetings and very thin written agreements as the norm on the Japanese side.'

Indeed, the Japanese tend to prefer brief, written contracts that outline the general principles of the agreement, and rely more on interpersonal trust for enforcement than legal proceedings. The level of detail expected in meetings and negotiations, then, is an important aspect of building mutual understanding of the issues and terms.

continues

continued

Table 6.1 Cultural approaches to meetings and negotiations.

Japanese	Cultural assumption	Americans	Cultural assumption
Many delegates		Few delegates	
	Collectivisim		Individualism
Decision-making based on group consensus		Decision-making based on compromise, majority voting, 'gut' feeling	
Formal conduct; little show of emotions	Neutral	Informal conduct; expressive	Affective
Indirect in speech	High-context communication	Direct in speech	Low-context communication
Agreements based on trust and mutual respect	Particularist and diffuse	Agreements based on legal agreements and rules	Universalistic and specific

This difference is also apparent in the differing practices of who attends negotiations. Americans are much more likely to send a very limited number of people who will be from corporate staff, perhaps accompanied by a legal adviser. The Japanese, on the other hand, are more likely to send a larger number of representatives who will have operational responsibility. So, while the operational people from Japan may want to go into great detail about operational issues in order to assess the alliance's potential, the Americans may want to talk numbers and about the various possibilities in terms of structuring the 'deal'.

Furthermore, the styles of negotiators are typically very different. The American style of negotiating is characterized by individual 'movers' who are assertive and outgoing – all qualities respected in a US business context. The Japanese style is characterized by formal conduct and politeness, avoiding direct confrontation or open displays of emotion. While Japanese have a much more complex, subtle style of communication, Americans are more expressive and concrete in their communication.

Practices for staff reward and promotion

There were also differences in the human resource practices between the two companies and cultures (see Table 6.2). For example, promotion at Toshiba was based more on seniority than on individual performance. Only at very senior levels in the organization did performance influence compensation. At Motorola, though, individual performance was used as a measure for promotion.

continues

continued

Table 6.2 Cultural approaches to HRM.

Japanese	Cultural assumption	Americans	Cultural assumption
Promotion and rewards based on seniority	Ascriptive orientation	Promotion and rewards based on individual achievements	Achievement orientation
Loyalty and mutual obligation characterize relationship between employer and employee	Diffuse and collectivist	Contractual, economic arrangement characterizes relationship	Specific and individualist

Integrating the cultures

Even before the joint venture was established, the cooperation and integration of the two cultures began. During the initial discussions, the two companies formed a joint task force to explore the potential for cooperation and success. The joint team was expected to review various aspects of the potential alliance and report back to the negotiators with their findings and recommendations. Once it was decided to move ahead, the composition of the management team for the joint venture was negotiated based on the complementary strengths of each company. Because Toshiba brought the process and memory competencies to the alliance, the president would be from Toshiba. For the other senior management positions, appointments were made from the parent that had a particular competency in the function. In addition to a shared management team, each parent company sent about 100 employees. Most of the employees sent from Motorola came from Nippon Motorola, many of whom were Japanese. American and British employees were also sent.

Mr Shima was very clear about the first actions to take: 'The very first policy was to establish the TSC [Tohoku Semi-Conductor] Management Philosophy. I told every person, "You are not Toshiba, you are not Motorola, YOU ARE TOHOKU."' He clarified the priorities and allegiances that managers and employees should have. The considerations should be in the following order:

1st position: TOHOKU
2nd position: MOTOROLA (your partner's position)
3rd position: TOSHIBA (your own parent company's position)

Explaining why this was important, Mr Shima said:

'It is very important for a joint venture to be relatively independent. Of course, you will always have demands on the joint

continues

continued

venture from the parent companies, and that is ok. But parent companies should think of the joint venture as a kind of customer. It is like our own parents. Every individual has parents that we may resemble physically, but we have our own ways of doing things. We need to develop our own personalities.'

The second action of the joint venture was to set out how to balance the 'Three Cs' of the alliance. (The phrase 'Three Cs' was coined by Business International in a 1987 study of competitive alliances. It referred to criteria for partner selection: Compatibility, Capability and Commitment.) At Tohoku, CC&C stands for Competition, Cooperation and Complementary. The policy that Mr Shima established to do this was really an attitude: To Respect, To Trust and To be Patient. This he made an explicit part of the company's philosophy (see Figure 6.2).

A third important action was to form joint task forces and project teams with representatives from both cultures. Whenever issues came up where each side had a different view of how something should be done, they formed joint teams to work out the best approach required to achieve company objectives and to report their suggestions to the board.

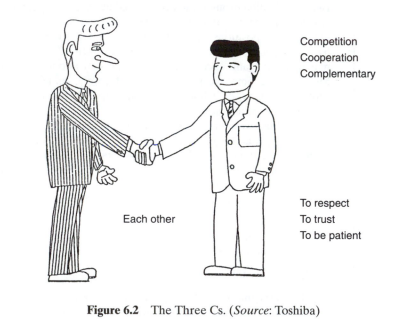

Competition
Cooperation
Complementary

Each other

To respect
To trust
To be patient

Figure 6.2   The Three Cs. (*Source*: Toshiba)

continues

continued

Mr Timmins's advice on managing the cultural differences that inevitably arise in cross-border alliances was:

(1) Try to understand why the other person thinks the way they do. You can get that through books, consultants, case studies, and so on. Invest the time to get to know the culture prior to doing business there.

(2) Understand the strategic reasons for the joint venture or alliance from both parties' perspectives. It helps to explain a lot of future actions and decisions.

(3) PATIENCE, PATIENCE AND PATIENCE. It takes a lot of time and effort to deal with people who are different. But it is worth it.

Both sides agreed on the other qualities of the joint venture that continue to make it a success:

- Proper employees (both companies sent senior employees, and the selection process is a careful one).
- Open access and support by both parent companies at senior levels;
- Relationship with employees – an employee association is involved in decision-making in the company.
- It was created to be a win-win relationship from the start; a 50:50 joint venture was really required ('Part of the philosophy was our responsibility to increase people's self-respect and harmony. An equal partnership went along with this').
- Making people feel as if they were part of the alliance from the start – they were TOHOKU, not Toshiba or Motorola.

The interaction between national and corporate culture

Where companies come together, it is often the case that the national *and* corporate cultures each contribute their own potential for creating mischief. It was Hofstede's belief that the national cultural dimensions he calibrated with IBM represented differences in work values. These, he insisted, were not factors that an organization could change, but were givens. The scores had to be seen as central tendencies. Not all Frenchmen have a higher power distance than Swedes, but the chances are that if a company hired locals in Paris, they would, on the whole, be less likely to challenge hierarchical power than would the same number of locals hired in Stockholm.

Challenged to identify what constituted corporate culture, Hofstede was stimulated to embark on a study of 20 organizational units in the

Netherlands and Denmark. They ranged from a police service, through an airline front desk, to a research laboratory. Hofstede postulated that organizations may differentially select for values (as Ikea does) or for locations where a bias exists within the labour population which can be expected to favour them. However, corporate culture is created through practices.

In joining organizations, employees learn quickly what rules are in place and which, if followed, will bring rewards. In PepsiCo, successful people must show cheerful, positive, enthusiastic, committed optimism. In Ford they must show self-confidence, assertiveness and machismo. These are the components of corporate culture. Professor Hofstede's research now forms the early database of a set of proprietary culture analysis techniques and programmes called DOCSA (Diagnosing Organizational Culture for Strategic Application, a proprietary cultural diagnostic process). The study revealed six dimensions, which are outlined in Table 6.3.

Table 6.3 The six dimensions of corporate culture.

Motivation	
Activities	*Outputs*
To be consistent and precise. To strive for accuracy and attention to detail. To refine and perfect. Get it right.	To be pioneers. To pursue clear and compelling aims and objectives. To innovate and progress. Go for it.
Relationship	
Job	*Person*
To put the demands of the job before the needs of the individual.	To put the needs of the individual before the demands of the job.
Identity	
Corporate	*Professional*
To identify with and uphold the expectations of the employing organization.	To pursue the aims and ideals of each professional practice.
Communication	
Open	*Closed*
To stimulate and encourage a full and free exchange of information and opinion.	To monitor and control the exchange and accessibility of information and opinion
Control	
Tight	*Loose*
To comply with clear and definite systems and procedures.	To work flexibly and adaptively according to the needs of the situation.
Conduct	
Conventional	*Pragmatic*
To put the expertise and standards of the employing organization first. To do what we know is right.	To put the demands and expectations of customers first. To do what they ask.

Box 6.3   Cultural comparisons between a Californian high-tech company and its European subsidiary

A successful US company had acquired a small company and subsequently launched into Europe through the UK. Within a few years, 40% of the revenues were earned outside the USA. But there were problems of communication and collaboration. A series of workshops in the UK were preceded by a questionnaire derived from the DOCSA corporate culture dimensions shown in Table 6.3.

The results are shown in chart form in Figure 6.3. It clearly shows a wide perceived difference in corporate culture. Europeans saw themselves as hard working, programmed and exploited. In contrast they saw their American colleagues as free spirits, loved by the company, and having none of the structured, head-down conscientiousness of their subsidiary units. The biggest concern for this organization was their consistently non-pioneering, non-pragmatic expression – highly worrying for a company whose success depends upon scientific innovation in a fiercely competitive environment.

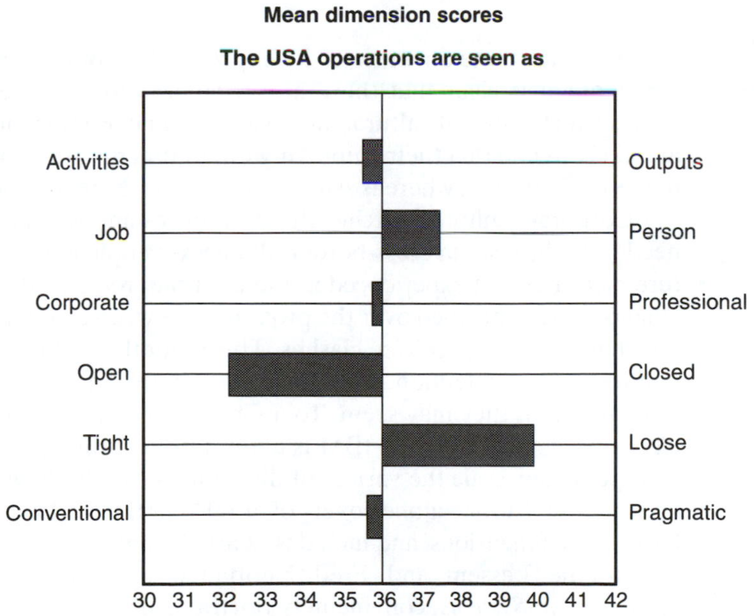

Mean dimension scores

The USA operations are seen as

Activities	Outputs
Job	Person
Corporate	Professional
Open	Closed
Tight	Loose
Conventional	Pragmatic

30 31 32 33 34 35 36 37 38 39 40 41 42

Figure 6.3   Corporate culture profiles.

continues

continued

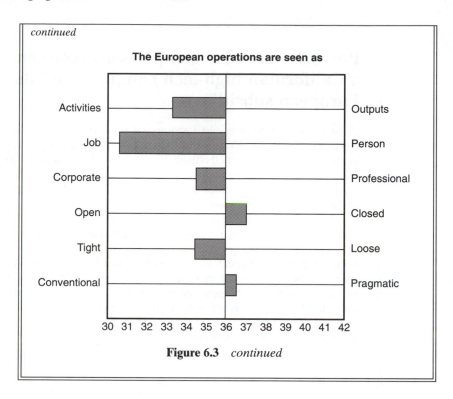

The European operations are seen as

Figure 6.3   *continued*

Although these dimensions are expressedly about typical observable behaviour it is clear that there are parallels with the prevailing work values which national cultural dimensions define. For example, Germans are likely to find that their employing environments are more 'Activities' in their orientation, whereas Americans will be more 'Outputs' oriented.

Corporate culture stretches the differences and widens the gaps that need to be bridged in cross-border alliances. People new to national culture measures, but experienced in the cultural problems that spring from alliances, are concerned over the proximity between country scores where they have seen huge culture clashes. This is another factor about cultures that needs close attention – the rule of proximity. The nearer they are the more different they may seem. To a Chicagoan, a New Yorker can seem like a foreigner. To Apple, IBM is alien. Looking through the nations of Europe on any scale the variety of differences clearly shows the range to be immense. Europe alone covers over 60% of the worldwide variance in Hofstede's dimensions, and includes nearly 50 linguistic minorities.

Ronnie Lessem and Fred Neubauer, in their book *European Management Systems*, convincingly portray Europe as offering four distinct ways of dealing with the world, based on the UK, France, Germany and Italy (Lessem and Neubauer, 1994). They see all kinds of parallels, each of which add weight to the casual belief that there is no way that these different countries could work in unison (see Table 6.4).

Table 6.4 European management characters.

Dimension	Characteristic			
	Western	*Northern*	*Eastern*	*Southern*
	UK	France	Germany	Italy
Corporate	Commercial	Administrative	Industrial	Familial
Managerial attributes				
Behaviour	Experiential	Professional	Developmental	Convivial
Attitude	Sensation	Thought	Intuition	Feeling
Institutional models				
Function	Salesmanship	Control	Production	Personnel
Structure	Transaction	Hierarchy	System	Network
Societal ideas				
Economics	Free market	Dirigiste	Social market	Communal
Philosophy	Pragmatic	Rational	Holistic	Humanistic
Cultural images				
Art	Theatre	Architecture	Music	Dance
Culture	Anglo-Saxon	Gallic	Germanic	Latin

They optimistically offer a way of reaching for a solution:

Having differentiated between pragmatic, rational, holistic and humanistic approaches, we then need, as managers and as firms, to integrate. Such integration, as we have seen, represents, on the one hand, a process of managerial and corporate individuation, and, on the other, one of individual and organizational learning. In effect, as Peter Senge at MIT has pointed out in his book *The Fifth Discipline* (published in 1992 by Century Business), such organizational learning is a composite of experientially oriented 'personal mastery', professionally based 'mental modelling', developmentally oriented 'systems thinking', and convivially based 'team learning', all of which together contribute towards a shared business vision.

From the perspective adopted in this book each of these four European domains is suffering from its undue isolation, excessive differentiation or, to put it nicely, its 'overdone strength'. While the pragmatic British suffer from their rampant shorttermism, and the rational French from their excessive bureaucracy, the holistic Germans are inclined to 'over-engineer' their products, and the humanistic Italians are prone towards nepotism. Each needs the other to 'individuate' culturally and economically, and such smaller countries as the Benelux and the Scandinavian nations have a vital role to play in fostering such integration.

Even where countries might be expected substantially to share their cultural imperatives, such as Spain and France, both seen as Latin and Catholic, they need to tread very carefully where there are negotiations about changes in corporate ownership. Case 6.2 illustrates this.

Case 6.2   Acquisition of Kyat (Spanish) by Syseca (French)

Syseca is a wholly owned subsidiary of the French company Thomson CSF, which specializes in information systems and services. Syseca has $220 million in annual sales and 2300 employees, and is managed by the Information Systems Group of Thomson.

In 1990 Syseca began exploring acquisition opportunities in Spain. The company targeted Kyat, a well-established Basque information services company with 250 employees and approximately $11 million in annual sales. Kyat was a well-run organization with operations in several cities throughout Spain.

To the lead negotiator, Robert Fillias, vice-president of International Subsidiaries for Syseca, Kyat seemed a good strategic fit. Some of the cultural differences that had to be managed in the negotiations, though, required much more than a purely financial and legal perspective.

Mr Fillias explained that to the Spaniards the negotiation process was really not about reaching an agreement and signing a contract. They first had to be sure that a solid basis of friendship had been established between the parties. This included ensuring that both sides shared the same fundamental values of trust and honesty. They wanted to take as much time as was necessary to get to know each other socially. Initial negotiations turned into a lengthy courtship, taking much longer than Mr Fillias was accustomed to. Furthermore, the discussions often turned to issues that were less 'objective', 'concrete' and strategic, and more subjective, general and relational.

> 'The Spaniards and the Basques wanted to be understood not so much to have their perspectives in the written contract, but they wanted us to remember what was important to them. They tried to ensure that we understood and shared their feelings on a number of things. Then they would feel comfortable that they would not be left in "alien hands".'

After a lengthy negotiation process, a contract was signed and the acquisition was successful. Key in the process, according to Mr Fillias, was appreciating the different cultural orientation of the other party rather than becoming frustrated. In his opinion it was important to try to adapt in order to build the trust and relationship that would eventually make the acquisition a success.

Although the differences between the French and Spanish are not large in terms of the cultural dimensions presented in Chapter 2, the differences did influence the way that both sides were accustomed to negotiating (see Box 6.4).

Box 6.4   Cultural approaches to negotiations

French	Spanish
'A meeting of minds'	'A meeting of people'
Rhetorical, Cartesian, intellectual	Personal, relationship orientation
Importance of intellectual competence	Importance of social competence
Persuasion through carefully prepared, skilful rhetoric	Persuasion through emotional appeal
Logical presentation of your position – negotiation is treated as a search for well-reasoned, detailed solutions	Socializing before getting down to business is important – negotiation is a forum for exchange of 'grand ideas' and general principles
Contract = well-reasoned transaction	Contract = long-lasting relationship
Trust emerges slowly and is based on the evaluation of perceived status and intellect	Trust develops on the basis of frequent and warm interpersonal contact and transaction
Additional trust comes as proof justifies it	

Managing the process

The following is a set of rules which are all necessary if success is to be achieved in cross-cultural alliances.

- Before considering the alliance, take time to understand the other culture. Review books and other publications about the culture and how to do business with people from that culture. If possible talk to expatriates who have worked in the culture.
- Try to make cultural assumptions about negotiations explicit. Negotiating styles, strategies and tactics are shaped by culture. This affects how agreements are reached (verbal agreements versus formal contracts), the way trust is built (through friendship versus well-reasoned argument), tolerance of conflict, and so on.
- Choose a partner that has complementary management strengths as well as complementary technical or geographical strengths.
- Clarify each potential partner's strategic reasoning, expectations, short- and long-term perspectives and contingency plans.
- Clarify the priorities and allegiances of the newly formed alliance. Communicate the priorities to all members of the organization.

This will lead to cutting the risks of finding a sound partner to manageable size. However, the steps following agreement are just as vital.

- Ensure that the top team is made up of culturally aware managers who are trained to work in a multicultural team.
- Establish a unique culture and philosophy for the independent company. The new culture should not try to replicate that of either of the parent companies.
- Set up a communication system to deal with the conflicts that inevitably emerge during the integration phase. Appoint a group of people from both companies to act as mediators and 'cultural interpreters'.
- Form task forces and project teams with representatives from both cultures to explore operational issues, formulate solutions and encourage teamwork.
- Measure the culture as it is or as they are, using questionnaires that can show comparisons with similar companies. Determine what corporate culture profile is to be sought given the alliance's strategic objectives. Identify the behaviours that will be rewarded. Put in place public milestones. Celebrate achievements. Monitor and publish the attainment of the cultural goals.

Gerald Egan, in *Management Today* (April 1994), adds a contemporary summary of ways to 'cultivate culture' once the deal is done.

- Use strategy as a starting point: alliances offer an ideal opportunity to use a new strategy as the incentive and stimulus to encourage both sets of employees to focus on finding the way of working that backs the strategic intent.

- Use all the current approaches to change management; total quality, customer service, process re-engineering. These offer the opportunity to create meaningful projects that help get people working together.
- Use the reorganization as a lever to challenge the existing cultures – create new roles, shift people out of their positions. Create new teams.
- See the alliance as a crisis. Encourage adrenalin to flow. This will unfreeze the existing positions and allow new thinking to enter before refreezing takes place.
- Blitz the organization with training programmes that promote the new values and the future cultural target.
- Make big symbolic changes. Asea Brown Boveri chose English as its corporate *lingua franca*. CEO Percy Barnevik's newly formed company was a Swedish/German combination, but he felt English was the language that most effectively represented the communication medium he sought.

Alliances can and should profit from diversity by taking the best from each component culture, and creating a new, unique product from them all. In this way, the identity of the alliance is made secure, yet the relevance and connection it has to its outside worlds remain intact. It is always going to be hard to do, but the rewards can be immense.

References

Bleeke J. and Ernst D., McKinsey & Co. (1991). The Way to Win in Cross-Border Alliances. *Harvard Business Review*, November-December

Buchanan R. and Berman T., Bain & Co. (1992). Building Successful Partnerships. *Acquisitions Monthly*, April

Financial Times (1992). 18 November, p. 14

Lessem R. and Neubauer E. (1994). *European Management Systems*. London: McGraw Hill

Business International (1990). *Making Alliances Work: Lessons From Companies' Successes and Mistakes*. London: Business International.

Index

achievement-oriented cultures 46–7, 123
Adler, Nancy 54–6
address, forms of 7–8
advertising 92–111
    limited potential for global 98–100,
        101–3, 111
    local adaptation 97, 101, 103–6, 108,
        110–11
    problems of translation 93
affective cultures 43
Aga, Lasse (Elf Aquitaine) 64
alliances 136–53
    advantages of 136
    bridging of national and corporate
        cultures 145-51
    reasons for failure 136, 137–8, 139
    recommendations for success 138–9,
        151–3
    role of culture in 139–45
    Toshiba-Motorola case study 140–5
Americans 43, 45, 76
    approach to human resource
        management 142–3
    career perceptions 129–30
    contrast with Japanese 7–8, 84–9, 87,
        140–3
    executive in Paris 12–14
    view of European behaviour 16–17,
        147
    see also United States
Anglo-Dutch model of career
        development 125–6, 128
Anglo-Saxon culture 12, 68
    concept of human resource management
        in 113, 134
    defined 8–9
    selection methods 122
Aoi, Mr (Toshiba) 119

'Apollo syndrome' 115
ascriptive cultures 46–7, 123, 134
Asia 69
    collectivism 71, 73, 74–5
    cultural link with economic
        growth 74–5
    culture diversity across 14
    morality 10–11
    paternalism 73–4
    selection methods 122
assumptions, cultural 10, 14, 21, 25–6
    differences between Americans and
        Japanese 87
    and organizational structure 53–6, 63
Austria 35, 37

Bain & Company 137, 139
Bartlett, Christopher 51–2
Bedi, Hari 4, 11
Belbin, Meridith 115, 135
Bond, Michael 74–5
BP (British Petroleum) 28–9, 132
brands, marketing of 99–101, 103, 106
Brazil 35
British companies
    alliance with Italian company 18–20
    and cultural learning at Toshiba 81–4
    marketing in Japan 93–4
    merger with French 6
    see also United Kingdom
Bührmann–Tetterode (BT) Group 69, 70

career development 125–31
    cultural perception of 129–31
    organizational models 125–9
Carnaud 6
Carstedt, Goran 58, 59–60, 61, 62, 68
change, capability of 5, 25–7

Chinese 10, 37, 39, 71, 74
Cho, Fujio 85–6
CMB (Metal Box-Carnaud merger) 6
Colgate–Palmolive 95
collectivist cultures
　in Asia 71, 73, 74–5
　core values of power distance and 72
　versus individualist 35–6, 37, 42, 47
Colombia 74
contracts 41
corporate culture
　dangers of 57, 62
　dimensions of 146–8
　Ikea case study 57–60
　importance of flexibility 121–2
　interaction between national
　　and 145–51
　relationship to economic
　　performance 57, 62
cultural learning
　case studies 81–9
　obstacles to 79–80
　required for cultural synergies 80–1, 90
　socialization of individual 25–6, 48
cultural mismanagement, costs of 1, 5–7,
　21
culture
　concepts of 28
　convergence of 2–5
　definitions 24–5
　essence of 4
　layers of 25–7
Czech Republic 137

decision-making 42, 52
Denmark 31, 35, 146
Derr, Brooke 129
diffuse cultures 44–5, 68
DOCSA (Diagnosing Organizational
　Culture for Strategic
　Application) 146, 147
Doz, Yves 114–16, 120, 132–3, 135
dualities, balancing of 114–16, 120

Earley, Christopher 37
Eastern cultures 71
　holistic thinking 75, 132
　selection methods 122
　see also Asia
Eenhoorn, J. W. (Unilever) 96
Elf Aquitaine 62, 63–4, 66
Emerson Electric 65–6, 68
emotion, display of 43
ethics 11
Europeans
　differences between 148–51
　view of American behaviour 16–17, 147
Evans, Paul 114–16, 120, 132–3, 135

feminity 29, 37, 68
　and individualism scores 61

Fillias, Robert (Syseca) 150
France 6, 77, 127
　American executive in Paris 12–14
　career perceptions 130
　cultural approaches to
　　negotiations 149–51
　high-context culture 98
　marketing in 99
　organizational form of companies 35,
　　64, 66, 67
　selection methods 122–3
Fruythof, Norbert (Elf Aquitaine)
　64
Furuta, Nate (Toyota) 87–8

Germanic model of career
　development 126
Germany 35, 76, 149
　career perceptions 130
　and market research 105
　marketing in 98
　selection methods 122
　Siemens case study 77–9
　specific/diffuse relationships 44–5
Ghoshal, Sumantra 51–2
global marketing 94–5
　advertising see advertising
　harmonization of products 95
　impact of cultural differences on 92–3
　views on 96
global organizations see transnational
　organizations
global products
　different perceptions of 95, 97
　potential for 92–3, 95–7
　successful examples of 97
Greece 31
Gruppo GFT 96

Hampden-Turner, Charles 76–7
Heineken beer 101, 102–3
Heltman, Sam (Toyota) 7
high-context cultures 98
Hofstede, Geert 25
　and dimensons of work-related
　　values 27–39, 43, 47, 48, 145
　and link between economic growth and
　　collectivism 74–5
　study of corporate culture 145–6
Hong Kong 3, 31, 33, 35, 39
human resource management 113–14
　balancing opposing dualities 114–16,
　　120
　career development 125–9
　career perception 129–31
　Japanese/American approach to 142–3
　performance appraisal 131–3
　role of professionals in 133–4
　selection methods 122–4
　statement of values 116–20
Hungary 137

ICI (Imperial Chemical Industries)   18–20
Ikea   57–61, 62, 121, 124
India   9
individualism   29
  business areas affected by   36, 42
  core values of powder distance and   72
  defined   35
  and industrialization   4
  and masculinity/feminity scores   61
  scores   36
  versus collectivism   35–6, 37, 42, 47
individualist cultures   71
  career development in   125–6, 128
  differences in work ethos between
    collectivist and   37
  reward in   42
Indonesia   33, 35
intelligence tests   122, 123, 134
international organizations
  need for broader mind-set   50–1
  need for organizational change   51–2
  view of cultural diversity   55, 63
Ireland   35, 42
Israel   35
Israsena, Paron   4–5
Italy   43, 149
  alliance with British company   19–20

Japan   9, 14, 31, 76, 77
  and adoption of outside knowledge
    5
  approach to human resource
    management   142–3
  career development in   126–7, 129
  collectivist culture   42, 71, 74
  contrast with Americans   7–8, 84–9, 87,
    140–3
  cultural approach to
    meetings/negotiations   141–2
  emphasis on teamwork   131
  marketing in   93–4
  on responsibility   88–9
Japanese companies
  alliance between Toshiba and
    Motorola   140–5
  in United Kingdom   81–4
  in USA   84–9
Johnson, Michael   11–14
Johnson & Johnson   104–5
joint ventures
  Rank-Toshiba   81–4
  Toshiba-Motorola   140–5
  see also alliances

Kamprad, Ingvar (Ikea)   58
Knight, Charles (Emerson Electric)   65–6,
  68
Kotter, John   62
Kyat (Spanish company)   150

Lancaster, Neil (Rank-Toshiba)   83

Latin model of career
  development   127–8, 129
Laurent, André   4, 26, 129–31
leadership behaviour   3
Lessem, Ronnie   148–9
Lester, Tom   133–4
Levi Strauss jeans   95
Lintas advertising agency   99
Lloyd, Gregory   10
Lotus   116–17
low context cultres   98

McDonald's restaurants   2, 76
McKinsey & Co   15, 138–9
management development   125–9
market research   104–5
marketing, global *see* global marketing
Maruyama, M.   54–6
masculinity   29, 37
  business areas affected by   38
  and individualism scores   61
  scores   38
meanings
  culturally dependent   24
  intended and perceived   99–101
mergers *see* alliances
Metal Box Company   6
Mexico   35
Mikura, Masaki (Toshiba)   188
modes of thought   9
morality   10–11
motivation   42
Motorola   117–18
  alliance with Toshiba   140–5
multidomestic organizations   54–5, 69
multinational companies (MNCs)
  organizational priorities   51–2
  views of cultural diversity   55–6, 69

negotiations   42, 141–2, 151
Nestlé   96
Netherlands   29, 43, 146
  Bührmann-Tetterode case study   69, 70
  career perceptions in   130
Neubauer, Fred   148–9
neutral cultures   43
Norway   35

Oda, Kanji (Toshiba)   84–5
Ohmae, Kenichi (McKinsey & Co)   15, 96
O'Neill, Vincent (Siemens)   77–9, 121–2
organizations
  basic characteristics for survival   54
  conception of   33–5, 39
  configuraton and co-ordination
    mechanisms   67
  and cultural assumptions   53–6, 63
  culture of   62–8
  need for change   51–2
  structure of   31, 33, 35, 50–1
Osrin, Neville (Steelcase Strafor)   110

particularist cultures 123, 134
  business areas affected by 41
  versus universalist 41, 47, 68
paternalism 73–4
performance appraisal 131–3
Poland 137
Porter, Michael 18, 75, 96
Portugal 31, 35
power distance 54
  in achievement/ascriptive-oriented
      cultures 46–7
  in Asia 71, 73
  business areas affected by 31
  conceptions of 28–9, 30
  core values of individualism/collectivism
      and 72
  management implications 31–5
  scores 30
  and uncertainty avoidance scores 34,
      60
private space 44–5
Procter & Gamble 93–4
products, perception of 93, 95, 97, 100
professional/technical culture 62–4
promotion, cultural perception of 125–9
public space 44–5

Renault 24
Rivetti, Marco (Gruppo GFT) 96

Schutz, Alfred 9
selection, cultural methods of 122–4
Shell 124, 132
Shima, Mr (Motorola-Toshiba) 141,
      143–4
Siam Cement Group 4–5
Siemens 77–9, 121–2
Singapore 31, 33, 35
Spain
  cultural approaches to
      negotiations 149–51
specific/diffuse relationships 44–5
status
  in achievement/ascriptive-oriented
      cultures 46–7
Steelcase Strafor 110-11
Stevens, Owen James 33
Swadling, Dennis (Rank-Toshiba) 82
Sweden 37, 43
  cultural values 61–2, 68
  Ikea 57–61, 62, 121, 124
Switzerland 35
Syseca (French company) 150

Taguchi, Tadao (Toshiba) 7
teamwork 13, 115, 131, 135
technical/professional culture 62–4
Thailand 4–5
Timmins, Richard
      (Toshiba–Motorola) 141, 145

Toshiba
  America Inc 7
  commitment of 118–20
  Consumer Products 84–5
  Motorola alliance 140–5
  Rank-Toshiba joint venture 81–4
Toyota Motor Manufacturing 7, 127
  in United States 85–9
training 78, 126
translations, problems of 93
transnational organizations 21, 75–6, 124
  characteristics of 52
  need for change in cultural
      assumptions 75–6, 90
  organizational priorities 51
  and set of values 15, 120
  view of cultural diversity 55, 56
Trompenaars, Fons 39, 40–7, 48, 76–7

uncertainity avoidance 29, 43, 47, 54, 66
  business areas affected by 32
  defined 31
  management implications 31–5
  and power distance scores, 34, 60
  scores 32
Unilever Foods 96, 103–4, 108
Unisys Corporation 109-10
United Kingdom 35
  selection methods in 122–3
  see also Britain
United States 2, 3, 6–7, 31, 37, 62, 68
  Emerson Electric case study 65–6
  low-context culture 98
  organizational model 35, 66
  selection methods 124
  and universalism 76–7
  see also Americans
universalist cultures 123
  and United States 76–7
  versus particularist 41, 47, 68

values, cultural 26, 54
  differences 10–11, 21
  dimensions of differences 27–39
  statement of company 116-20
van Oordt, Robert (Bührmann-
      Tetterode) 70
van Os, Leo (Lintas Advertising) 99

Western cultures
  analytical thinking 75
  business practices 137
  contrast with Asia 71
  individulism 131–2
  management theories 8–9
Williams, George (Rank–Toshiba) 83–4
Williams, Jim (Young & Rubicam) 98, 99,
      104

Young & Rubicam (Y & R) 98, 99, 104